THIS
WORD
NOW

OWEN EGERTON · JODI EGERTON

Publication Note:
Some of these pieces, in slightly different forms, originally appeared in *The Huffington Post* as "Type So Hard You Bruise the Screen," "Write Like a Drunk Child," and "Damn the Writers."

ISBN: 978-0-692-72048-6

CONTENTS

THIS WORD NOW...5
WHO WE ARE...6
TYPE SO HARD YOU BRUISE THE SCREEN 7

WHERE DO YOU WANT TO BE?

HORIZONS AND LANDMARKS...15
SHARING THE SHELF...19

PLACE, TIME, RITUAL

COOKING THE KITCHEREE..25
PLACE..26
TIME..28
RITUAL...29
WRITING MOM...30
PUBLIC PING PONG..32
ANY WAY THAT WORKS...34
RELEASING AND WELCOMING..36
SENSES..38

EXPECTATIONS

LOWER YOUR EXPECTATIONS..43
RAISE YOUR EXPECTATIONS...45
MAPS AND BACKROADS..46

SURPRISE

THE BOUNCER IN MY BRAIN..53
SURPRISE..55

GATHERING FIREWOOD

FIRE 61
MINDMAPS 62
INSPIRATION JARS 64
CLIPPINGS 66

PRAYER SEX PLAY

WRITING AS PRAYER 73
WRITING AS SEX 74
WRITING AS PLAY 75
MUSIC 76

QUESTIONS, GHOSTS, AND HIDDEN STONES

REAL BRIGHT HARD 81
GHOSTS 83
CIRCLE THE QUESTIONS 84
REMEMBERING 86

TURNING THE HANDLE

THE WAY IN 91
MIX AND MATCH 97
BUG OFF 98
MUSEUM DISCOVERY 99
GENRE TOURISM 100

FIRESTARTERS

LIGHTING THE FIRE 105
LIGHTNING 106
BORROW A SPARK 107
LIGHTER FLUID 108
MAGNIFY 109
TWO STICKS 110
WILDFIRES 112

IN THE BEGINNING...

WARNING 117
BEGINNINGS 118
THE LOGIC OF DREAMS AND NIGHTMARES...122

TORTURE YOUR CHARACTER

OBSTACLES THAT DEMAND ACTION...129
THAT FISH CAN'T BREATHE..131
ODD COUPLING 133
NOPE..135
ELEVATOR 136

SUSPENSE!

MAKE YOUR READER HUNGRY...141
HITCHCOCK ON SUSPENSE AND SURPRISE...143
THE IMPOSSIBLE SITUATION 145
THE UNTHINKABLE THIRD...147
ALL THE OPTIONS 149

REALITY, NEEDS, AND SNAPS

EXPECTATION VS. ACTUALITY 155
NEED VS. WANT 157
SNAP!..159
SNAPS!...163

THE WHITE HOT HEART

FINDING THE HEART 169
FEED THE FIRE..170
FIGHT THE FIRE 172
TOO HOT TO TOUCH 174
COUNTDOWN 175

HAPPY ENDINGS AND COMPLEX CLIMAXES

ENDINGS 181
MARKING THE BEATS 185

REVISION AND WRITER'S BLOCK

PUT IT AWAY...191
MESSED UP DRAFT 192
THE POWER OF PLAY... 194
READ IT AGAIN FOR THE FIRST TIME 198

TINKERING, TWEAKING, AND POLISHING

DIVING BACK IN... 209
ONE IDEA, ONE PARAGRAPH... 210
CLEAR THE CLUTTER 212
THE JOY OF DELETE 213
REDUNDANCIES, REDUNDANCIES....................................... 215
DROP THAT 217
QUIT THE QUALIFIERS... 218
LESS IS MORE 219
DOWN TO SPECIFICS 221
TO BE OR NOT TO BE 222
IN DEFENSE OF PASSIVE VOICE.. 224
WE'RE HUNTING HABITS.. 225

ONWARDS

ARE YOU FINISHED? 231
GENIUS MEATBAG 233
PRAYER FOR WRITERS 235
ACKNOWLEDGEMENTS.. 239
ABOUT THE AUTHORS 241

THE RULES

1. *Have fun.*
2. *Believe in yourself.*
3. *Don't cheat.*
4. *Type in your code name.*
5. *Be awesome.*
6. *Always destroy your enemy with awesomeness.*

Oscar Egerton, age 6

There are three rules for writing a novel.
Unfortunately, no one knows what they are.

W. Somerset Maugham

THIS WORD NOW

You don't need this book.

You don't need an MFA degree or a traumatic childhood or an apartment in Greenwich Village or a subscription to *The Paris Review*. You don't need a mentor or more free time or a lucrative book deal. You don't need an agent or an office or an excuse. You don't need encouragement or inspiration. You don't need permission.

You don't need any of these things to write.

All you need is a word.

This word. The one your pen is touching. The one popping to the screen as you type. That thin-lined, mundane miracle. An image, an idea, an action, an imperfect something, a beginning.

That's all you need. This word now.

And because now is ongoing, so are the words.

This book rambles through the process. Warming up the words, hunting the storms, hammering the structure, and moving on. There are essays, observations, exercises, and confessions. We've gathered our own tools for creativity from years of writing, performing, and teaching, and collected some our favorite writers' and creatives' methods.

Our hope is that you put down the book often, so you can pick up a pen. In the metaphor of a campfire, we hope this book provides a few matches, maybe a squirt of lighter fluid or a hint of where to find a good supply of dry wood. If it comes down to it, rip out these pages and burn them as kindling.

Because you don't need this book.

All you need is this word now.

WHO WE ARE

When we met, we were already both enamored with creativity.

Jodi had deserted the northeast for the wilds of Austin to pursue a post-graduate degree in English and Rhetoric at the University of Texas. She balanced her academic days with play. Not long after moving to Austin, she auditioned for the city's top improv troupe. She'd been trained in classical clowning and performed improv in college at Swarthmore, and was already a stylized comedian.

Owen was living in a van. He quit his full-time job, moved into a 1975 VW Camper, and worked to complete his first novel. During the evening he scored enough comedy gigs to pay for food and gas and during the day he abused Austin coffee shops' bottomless cup policies and typed.

We met through comedy. We courted at Quackenbush's.

Our days were spent battling our way through books – Jodi's dissertation and Owen's first novel. Our weekends were packed with shows – making up scenes, songs, and one-liners on the spot. We filled our days with careful crafting and revision and our nights with public spontaneity. Ever since, our work, our romance, and our parenting have orbited these two poles. This book is no exception. We champion the dual disciplines of hard-won craftsmanship and childlike play. They are the ingredients of great art and great living and a great deal of fun.

We collaborated on every piece in this book. But some essays are more personal than others. When necessary we'll name the particular writer of a section. Otherwise, you can assume it was both of us. The insights we gathered from an extended family of creatives and a long lineage of artists. We owe a great deal to the writers, readers, teachers, clowns, musicians, tinkerers, crafters, seamstresses, parents, and children who inspire, support, and mentor us.

TYPE SO HARD YOU BRUISE THE SCREEN

1.   Write. Now. Go.

2.   Don't think. Scribble. Scribble. Scribble. Type so hard you bruise the screen.

3.   Now think.

4.   Revise. Revise. Revise. Cut. Cut. Cut. Rewrite. It is the sweat of craft.

5.   Don't always know what your images mean.

6.   Do always know what your sentences mean.

7.   Do not wait for inspiration. Go out and hunt it. Seduce it. Pin it down and dribble spit on its forehead until it cracks your leg bone and re-names you.

8.   Writing takes time. Don't find the time to write. Make the time. If necessary, abandon sleep, people, television, and drink.

9.   Treat writing like a hobby and you will receive nothing but the fruits of a hobby. It's a vocation. Honor it as such.

10. Don't say you're trying to be a writer. If you're writing, then you are a writer. Publication is nice, but has nothing to do with the definition.

11. Love rejection. In letters, in criticism, in sales. Rejection is evidence you are in the game. If you're striking out, it means you got up to bat.

12. Drink and talk with those that write and create, but never mistake talking about writing for actual writing.

13. Love solitude.

14. Celebrate arrogance. You're calling yourself a writer, for godsake. Embrace it.

15. A person can only read so many words in a lifetime. Your reader is choosing to read you instead of Shakespeare, Hemingway, Whitman. Humbly honor that and give them the best of your soul.

16. Do not write from answers. Write from questions. Discover more questions. Our work is not to explain the mystery, but to expand it.

17. The craft of the sentence is important. But a perfectly crafted sentence with no passion is a well-dressed corpse. More fun to dance with a beggar than kiss a corpse.

18. For a writer, the internet is more dangerous than whisky.

19. Whisky is pretty dangerous, too.

20. *Write what you know* is fine. But better to reach beyond what you know, grasp for what is beyond your reach.

21. The best fiction is magnificent failures. So fail magnificently.

22. If your story isn't worth telling a stranger in a bar, it's not worth writing.

23. In life many of us aim to avoid conflict. In fiction, we force enemies into a room with no doors.

24. Laugh out loud at your own written words. Even in public... Especially in public.

25. If you don't discover anything while writing, don't expect your reader to.

26. Dream onto the page. I mean dream in every sense of the word. Wishing. Fantasizing. And the unconscious game of your unthought thoughts bubbling into fragmented memories and shaping a narrative with elements of your life, but in a completely unexpected order and relationship.

27. Live well. If your life is dull, it will seep into your pages like a stench. Take long walks. Get lost. Read. Read. Look foolish. Kiss people on the mouth.

28. If you write because you believe the world needs you, you'll soon discover we don't. If you write because you are so naturally talented you must, you'll soon discover you are not. If you write for money... I'm chuckling at you. None of these reasons will sustain you. Listen. Are you called to write? Then write.

29. You are going to die. So are all your readers. Let this inform every story you write.

30. Writing is both holy and meaningless. That's all the pressure and freedom you need.

WHERE DO YOU WANT TO BE?

We are all apprentices in a craft where no one ever becomes a master.

Ernest Hemingway

HORIZONS AND LANDMARKS

What do you want to do as a writer? What's the goal? What's the dream? Write it down. Read it. Write it down again.

Don't do this with weak modesty. Write the big ones down, the ones co-workers and your aunt Betty would smirk at. Write down the shallow ones, too. Write them all down. You don't have to share this with a soul, except your own soul.

The directions of our lives are guided by what we desire, so craft your desires. Cultivate your dreams. Tend to your growing wants like vegetables in a garden. Because what you want will define what you work for and influence what you get.

Truth is, plenty of us get exactly what we want.

"I just want to get by." Guess what. You just get by.

"I'm just writing for fun. It doesn't matter if anyone reads it." Guess what, no one will.

HORIZON GOALS

One never reaches a horizon. As you move forward the goal recedes, the distance remains the same. The horizon is not a destination; it's a direction.

I'm going to be the finest writer I am capable of being.

I'll create works of beauty that entertain and inspire.

I'll live with compassion and love those around me.

These are important goals to write down and reread. Goals of spiritual enlightenment fall into a similar category. Some of these goals will stay with a person through a lifetime. They provide a direction.

LANDMARK GOALS

A Landmark Goal sets a destination, a concrete goal that can be achieved on the path to the Horizon Goal.

Do you want to write a book? Write it down. State it. Move toward it.

Do you want to publish the book? Write it down. Move toward it.

Do you want to win the Nobel Prize for literature? Write it down. Move toward it.

Of course, it's not all up to you. Publishers and the prize committees and such. You can't worry about them. You have to do your part. And the first step is writing it down.

QUESTION YOUR DREAM

Once you've written down your goal, take a close look. Question your wants.

Is it really your dream or have you just borrowed someone else's? A good friend kept being told by her agent that the big goal for her career was writing a literary novel that would wow academia and dazzle *The New York Times* reviewers. For a long time, she knocked her head against the pages trying to achieve this goal. In her free time, she wrote young adult stories she adored. It took her years to realize she didn't really want to pen the modern literary classic. She wanted a YA wonder! That's where she felt inspired. Once she was able to question her goals, she could move toward what she really wanted.

Is your *real* desire hiding underneath your goals?

A friend told me he wanted to be as rich as Oprah. When asked why, he answered that the money would allow him to work less. Why didn't he want to work? He wanted to spend as much time with his kids as he could before they grew up.

The Oprah money was a ruse. What he wanted, really wanted, was time with his kids. He could step in that direction without having the bank account of a billionaire media tycoon.

Now question how your Landmark Goals connect with your Horizon

Goals. Do they harmonize? Are they situated in the same direction?

If my Horizon Goal is writing a collection of beautiful, moving poetry, but my Landmark Goal is to make a million dollars no matter what the writing assignment entails, well, I may need to spend some soul time thinking about my goals.

COMPARE THE DREAM WITH THE DAY

Read those goals again. Now read your schedule for your day. Do they match up?

If you want to write a novel but you're not grabbing the time to write, you better rethink things. It's fine to point into the distance and say, "That's where I'm going," but it means nothing if you're standing still.

Take a look at your plans for this week, for the month, for the year. What's on your agenda? Does it match your bigger dreams? If not, make some changes. You can learn quite a bit about how you are spending your life by taking note of how you spend a day.

And if that Landmark Goal is too far away, find some landmarks in between. Number of pages written, finishing a draft, starting a draft. Set the goals that lead to where you want to be.

NO GUARANTEES

We are understandably afraid of voicing dreams—especially big ones. Once we name our dreams it will be impossible to deny if they don't come true. If we've written our dreams down, declared them as goals, we risk defined, undeniable failure.

Failing is part of the adventure. If you're achieving every goal you set, then you're setting the bar too low. You *should* be failing; you *should* be striving.

But it still hurts.

You write down your goals. You work toward them. You give it all your heart. And you may very well fail. There's no guarantee that you'll reach any of your goals. We know it, but we don't always *believe* it. Movies and pop songs preach that if you try hard enough, you'll reach that finish line. But that's not true.

Dreaming is much more dangerous than that. The game is not fixed, the ending is not secured, the risks are real. And worth it.

SHARING THE SHELF

Imagine your book at its best.

Through passion and revision, it has become what it wanted to be. Now imagine a reader who adores this book. She's finishing the last page now, sighing with wonder. If you were to ask her at this moment to name a favorite book of all time, it would be yours.

She stands from her chair to place your book among her other favorites of all time—a small shelf reserved for her most loved authors.

Who else is up there? Who do you share a shelf with?

This is no time for humility. Aim big. It's a mental exercise to discover what tradition you're writing in. What's your literary family tree? What books share DNA with yours?

Is Virginia Woolf your grandmother?

Is Franz Kafka your cousin?

Do Alice Walker and Robert Ludlum come over for Thanksgiving?

Perhaps you enjoy the bite and grin of Kurt Vonnegut and Mark Twain. Or you're more interested in the dark corners of crime along with James Ellroy and Jim Thompson. Or do you write twisted myths like Aimee Bender and Kelly Link?

This doesn't mean you're copying these writers; it means you're related. Knowing your family, knowing with whom you share a shelf, helps you know something about your book and about you. Study them. How did your fellow writers do what you're trying to do? Where did they fail?

Again, this is not a suggestion to let your voice succumb to another's. You are your own writer. No one could ever imitate you and you can never fully imitate another writer. If you were to try to rewrite Charles Dickens' *Oliver Twist* you couldn't help but make it your own. Your voice is as distinct as a fingerprint. But it is related to those who came before.

None of us write in a vacuum. We are part of a living tradition, an ongoing conversation, a family. In what is often a lonely practice, this can be a great comfort. And also a challenge. If Stephen King is your older brother, you've got a lot to write up to. But you can do it. It's in your DNA.

PLACE,
TIME,
RITUAL

A writer who waits for ideal conditions under which to work will die without putting a word on paper.

E.B. White

COOKING THE KITCHEREE

JODI

On this slow Sunday morning, I'm cooking a hearty batch of kitcheree—healing, spiced rice and mung beans—a favorite recipe shared by my midwife. Unlike my usual slap-dash quick dinners, this recipe moves slowly, each step requiring a half hour or more to absorb water, simmer, cook.

It's so easy to forget, to leave the stove going, walk away and get distracted, lost in tasks, in work, in laundry. But don't forget, because it'll burn, because it'll turn bitter.

It takes mindfulness. It's a craft. It needs you, it needs your presence. And you will be rewarded. The house smells like curry and each bite is otherworldly. It's a feast flavored by your investment, your time, your patience, and presence.

PLACE

OWEN

An oak desk in a book-lined study. The kitchen table. A corner of a local coffee shop. For some it's the same space every day—a room reserved solely for the act of writing. For others, like myself, it's a rotating collection of spots scattered across the city.

Memoirist Sarah Hepola writes in bed, covers pulled to her neck so that she feels safe, alone, and able to write with the intimacy of a diary entry. While living with her young children and husband in Maine, Amanda Eyre Ward rented a hotel room for a summer to complete a novel. Toni Morrison is also a fan of hiding away in a hotel room with her manuscript. A lover's nook—hidden from the world—where sounds, smells, secrets can be shared.

Find what works, even if it doesn't fit your expectations. Stephen King wrote at the kitchen table until his early success afforded him a beautiful, wood desk. He sat at that desk in his study, the perfect picture of a writer and felt...wrong. He was back at the kitchen table within the hour.

My favorite is the southeast corner of the deck behind Once Over Coffee Bar on South 1st Street in Austin, Texas. In the shade of live oaks with Bouldin Creek babbling below me and a hot cup of coffee before me, I dive into the words. Others work or chat around me and I'm comforted by the white noise of their conversations. I feel alone and together.

My other favorite spot is the shed behind our house. As our family grew, I lost the luxury of a study. I pulled my secondhand desk out to the shed and set up a writing spot. It's musty and dusty. The wood walls are rotting and don't do much to keep out the rain or wind. Sometimes a possum pokes its head in to see what I'm up to or a stray cat jumps down from the rafters. I love the space. I love its separation from the duties and distractions of the house. I love the quiet. I love how alone I am in that space (except for the possum). It's strange and holy, like a small chapel or a monk's cell set aside for prayer. In that shed I type and wrestle. I cry onto my laptop. I giggle aloud.

Find your space or spaces. And if you don't find it, make it. Honor the space. Good things will come to be here.

TIME

Early morning before the first hint of sun. Midday, when the kids are at school and the house is quiet. All night at a twenty-four-hour diner.

Amelia Gray loves the early writing, sometimes scribbling stories before she's fully awake, allowing her dream logic to lead the way. K. A. Holt waits until the kids are asleep, then spreads her pages across the living room floor.

Like your space, let the time be strange and holy—dedicated to the writing. Turn off the phone. Turn off the internet. Some writer friends use programs which disable their internet for an allotted space of time every day. Other writers have just ripped the modem right out of the laptop.

If you don't have the time, find it, steal it, crack open the day and discover the hidden hours. Abandon television. Cut out drinking. Wake up an hour earlier. Faulkner worked as a night watchman, secretly writing *As I Lay Dying* when he was supposed to be watching the University of Mississippi power plant.

Writing will and should make demands of you. Like any relationship, it asks for hours, for headspace, for heart. If you never make plans to meet your lover, there's a good chance you never will. If, when seated across from your lover in some secluded corner of a café, you continue to check your email and Twitter, then you will have a less-than-stellar date. If you only see your lover if she calls, if she tugs at your heart, then, I believe, she will seek out a more devoted companion.

Honor the time. Demand that others honor it. Good things will come to be in these hours.

RITUAL

You've got your space. You've got the time. Now, how do you enter into the page? For some it's a first sip of coffee and three deep breaths. Others read the entire morning paper. Victor Hugo would down two raw eggs and often remove all his clothes before putting pen to paper. Colette would pick the fleas off her dog as a way of preparing to write. Friedrich Schiller filled a drawer of his desk with rotten apples, believing the smell inspired his best work.

Some light candles, welcoming the writing hours like the Sabbath. Others pray or meditate. Some complete *The New York Times* crossword. For others it's a poem. Something by Carrie Fountain or Rumi or Charles Bukowski. Slowing the eyes and quickening the mind.

Your ritual can be as simple as one full-body stretch, a taste of lemon water, a certain coffee mug, slippers, a mantra, a song. Find a way to mark the moment, to pronounce to yourself that this time and space have been set aside for the pursuit of words.

Honor your ritual. And by doing so, honor your writing.

A place, a time, and an opening ritual help frame your writing work. It is a way of respecting your craft. You are gifting the craft space, hours, heart. And the craft will reciprocate. You are protecting a time, space, and intention. Good things await.

WRITING MOM

JODI

Owen gifted me with a long weekend writing retreat. The plan was simple: I would hole up in a borrowed condo with a friend who was also under a writing deadline. We'd write straight for two solid days and leave triumphant and sated.

The reality looked a little different. Within hours of arriving on Friday, Owen checked in that Arden, our almost-ten-year-old, was rocking a high fever. Normally this wouldn't shake up a writing retreat, but that night the crew was supposed to go camping and then wake up the next morning and join a park ranger on a project to catch, band, and release birds.

This trip was a dream come true for six-year-old Oscar. Since he was two, Oscar's been on a mission to catch a bird. He's gotten way too good at sneaking up on seagulls and pigeons, and I've harbored a deep, nagging worry that at some point he really will catch a bird…and what then? So this trip, it was meant for Oscar.

But Arden was sick. And Owen hated having to bother me, but parenting really does trump all else, and we had to brainstorm.

We came up with multiple contingency plans. I would work until it was time for them to leave for the campground, and then I'd head home and hope that Arden was content to watch movies while I tried to keep writing. Or I'd stay overnight and they'd cancel the camping, but I'd return home at the crack of dawn so the boys could head off and catch birds.

Any plan basically sucked. Any plan was going to derail my writing retreat. But there didn't seem to be any good option.

This story has multiple happy endings. Owen reported in the morning that Arden slept hard and woke up feeling great. And in the time between hearing she had a fever and hearing that the fever was gone, I wrote two thousand words.

They were frantic words, and not my best words, but hot damn if I didn't write with a fire under me.

PUBLIC PING PONG

You hop online, promising you just need to look up the name of the fourth president of the United States of America. An hour later you're neck-deep in eighteenth century wig manufacturing, sucked in a fascinating never-ending information vortex known as the internet.

Writers are well aware that the internet, for all its wonders, can be an utter time suck. But that's just the tip of it. It's not only the minutes (or hours) we spend when we leave our writing and check our email, it's the change in our mindset.

PING PONG

When you click onto Facebook or Twitter or Instagram, you are immediately jumping into a game of ping pong. A comment comes your way and you like it or retweet it, smacking it like a lightweight plastic ball. Someone comments on your comment, and the rally continues. It feels so yummy for a writer who spends hours in isolation to step into the crowded game room of the internet.

The ideas and witty comments get bounced around for a few minutes. But when you return to the novel, you've lost the groove. No one is liking that brilliant last sentence of yours. No one has shared that wonderful insight. No one is commenting. You're serving ball after ball—but no one is hitting back. And you're waiting for something to react to, something to comment on, something to reply to.

As opposed to the more meditative state of writing, social media pulls us into a crowded conversation. We swim up from the deeper waters and get a breath of fresh air in the sunny shallow seas. Nothing wrong with that, except it takes quite a bit of effort and time to swim back down. It's tempting to stay splashing with the crowd in the warm surface waters. Plenty of small fish up here, but they're tiny. We're hunting mackerels.

NAKED IN PUBLIC

Writing can be lonely. In fact, it should be lonely. We need a certain solitude to explore and craft. But when we log on, we're on a stage before millions. It's part of the temptation. The instant gratification of a well-worded tweet is stiff competition for the drudgery of working on a long piece that may or may not ever be read.

We are constantly reminded that the second we type a word online it belongs to the world. It's become second nature to be careful with our words, thoughtful and cautious. Thoughtful and cautious works for social media, dinner table conversation, and political speeches, but it is the death of a first draft. A writer needs the freedom of not being read—the freedom to write the unreadable. It's easy to slip into the mindset that our words will be published as soon as we press return. A terrifying prospect.

Write naked. Post clothed.

SO WHAT DO WE DO?

First, observe yourself. Take note when you have the urge to check your email or Instagram. Does the urge hit when you're stumped by a sentence or section of your writing? Does the temptation grow stronger the longer you stay away? Or do you submerge into the work at hand?

Second, make a plan. Give yourself the gift of a few hours with no internet. If that's tough, try one hour. Turn the wi-fi off, so if you want to get online you have to go through some steps as opposed to the usual thoughtless click.

Third, stay with the work. Stay in the waters. Type away. And even when the words fail, stare at the screen and move through the doldrums. Those wordless hours are also writing. Don't miss it.

ANY WAY THAT WORKS

Let's follow up all this advice with the reminder that whatever works works.

Some are monastics, waking before the sun, retreating to a cell, study, or deserted kitchen, opening up their laptops or notebooks and writing in a quiet void. Their spot and hours are set and sacred.

Others are word counters. One thousand words a day no matter what. Ray Bradbury wrote *Fahrenheit 451* on a rented typewriter—10 cents every half hour. He was poor enough that each dime mattered and the pressure helped heat his already boiling imagination.

Others are haphazard, writing when the spirit moves them, scribbling phrases and plots on the back of napkins and the inside of matchbooks. Poet Ruth Stone talks of working in the field, feeling a poem coming like a fierce wind. She'll rush back home, racing in front of the poem so she can have pen in hand as the poem moves through her. If she's too slow, the poem blows on and finds another pen.

Writer Christie Grimes bases her writing schedule on the wisdom of master violinist Jascha Heifetz, who said, "If I don't practice one day, I know it; two days, the critics know it; three days, the public knows it."

On the other hand, George Saunders once eased the worries of a younger writer who was not writing every day by assuring her that sometimes the kettle is full but not yet boiling. It's okay to wait.

Some write with such painful ferocity that we stand in awe, envy, and a little horror. Jack Kerouac typed madly for three weeks on one long, continuous scroll so he wouldn't have to replace the paper in his typewriter. Honoré de Balzac drank gallons of coffee while desperately scratching out masterpiece after masterpiece. Amazing. But of course Kerouac destroyed his body with drink and uppers. And Balzac ran himself to an early death like a rider whipping a horse to run until its legs break.

Want to know the correct way of building a writing process? Any way that works. How one courts the muse is personal and unique writer to writer. Do not buy into someone else's process. There are as many writing processes as there are writers.

This is your craft. Your process. Your words.

RELEASING AND WELCOMING

JODI

We'd just returned back to Austin after seven months living in Los Angeles, and I was gifted with two nights away as a way to reconnect, rejuvenate, and rediscover myself. As I arrived at the retreat center, I discovered a labyrinth tucked in a corner of the grounds.

I love the meditative nature of a labyrinth—while it looks like a maze, it's not a puzzle to sort. There's only one direction, inwards, and there's nothing to do but put one foot in front of the other. The beauty of the labyrinth lies in its design—often you feel like you must be nearly to the center, only to find yourself on the far outskirts of the pattern. Eventually you arrive in the middle, and upon pausing to reflect on your success, realize that you must now turn around and repeat the journey outwards.

I am not a natural meditator. I don't like sitting still, and I rarely find quiet in my mind. A labyrinth is the perfect way to find stillness in motion. And as I discovered the releasing and welcoming exercise, I found a way for the journey of the labyrinth to be a gateway into my retreat weekend.

On the way into the labyrinth, I began releasing. Releasing anything that felt stuck in my head. Releasing worries. Releasing stress. Releasing school lunches. Releasing credit card debt. Releasing doctor's appointments. Releasing oil changes. As I spoke each item aloud, my brain let it go—I met it, acknowledged it, and released it. When I found myself stuck for ideas, I'd just repeat "Releasing, Releasing," until another worry popped into my mind.

I reached the center of the labyrinth, and breathed. Then I turned to head out. Once I reached the end, I'd be fully immersed in my retreat, and I knew it was time to open myself to the goodness that lay ahead of me.

I followed the path out of the labyrinth, and I began welcoming. Welcoming calm. Welcoming deep sleep. Welcoming slow mornings. Welcoming creative rejuvenation. Welcoming tasty meals, eaten slowly. Welcoming play.

As I exited the labyrinth, I checked in with myself. I felt great. Energized, yet relaxed. Refreshed. Even more, the nagging voice nudging me to take care of bills, to check things off of my to-do list…was quiet. I felt stillness, and I was able to move forward into my weekend.

Now I use Releasing and Welcoming as a warm-up exercise to start my writing sessions. Sometimes it's as simple as jotting down the items on my to-do list and making a quick note of my main goal for the day. As soon as they're written down, my brain releases the list items and welcomes the goal.

You can do this exercise in any medium you like—you can write long-hand, you can type, you can speak it aloud, you can jot it down on paper, you can take a walk and send each item to the trees you pass. Once you've released them, you're free to write.

SENSES

Check in with each of your five senses. This is an exercise we often use to start writing workshops. It's meditative and grounding, and will help you leave the chatter behind and focus.

What do you see?

What do you hear?

What do you taste?

What do you smell?

What do you feel?

Write for equal time on each. One minute, two minutes, five minutes. Just focus on that sense. What are you hearing? What else are you hearing? Listen underneath that sound, and find another sound you're hearing. Focus your attention on the sense, let the words flow where they will.

Pay attention to the stuff that's usually white noise. Turn off your internal editor. Don't correct, don't rewrite, don't rephrase. Just check in with your body and its experience sensing the world.

EXPECTATIONS

I wanted a perfect ending. Now I've learned, the hard way, that some poems don't rhyme, and some stories don't have a clear beginning, middle, and end. Life is about not knowing, having to change, taking the moment and making the best of it, without knowing what's going to happen next.
Delicious Ambiguity.

Gilda Radner

LOWER YOUR EXPECTATIONS

The blank screen screams. The book, story, essay, poem could be anything. You sit and stare out into a world that has yet to be. The endless possibility is exhilarating and, all too often, paralyzing.

Right now, before you've typed a single word, the story has the possibility of being perfect. Perhaps the idea of the story is already in your head—a glimmering, hot gem of an idea, begging to be manifested by a master with just the right words, just the right tone. Perfect, brilliant pages. All you have to do is write one perfect word after another after another after another. That's all.

Crap.

Few things imprison a writer more than the false call of perfection.

In order to reach beauty, we have to write ugly, knowing that the finished draft waits on the other side of a dozen or more imperfect drafts.

Writers lie to themselves—*the first draft will be perfect! From God's mouth to my pen. Not a word needs changing.*

Go ahead and believe it. For now.

It eases the frustration.

Poet Carrie Fountain has a note card pinned above her desk, quoting William Stafford: "LOWER YOUR EXPECTATIONS"

You don't need to write the perfect sentence. You need to write a sentence. That's your job right now. Words on the page.

As soon as you type a single word something terrifying happens. A thousand possible books die. You've taken a path, which necessarily means you are not taking another path. For those of us who long to do everything all the time, this can be heart-wrenching.

But when we begin to write, something amazing happens. The piece comes to be. The actualized story—written and printed—beats the fantasy of perfect possibilities every time.

You'll meet plenty of writers who don't write. You'll meet them at cocktail parties and in post office lines and they'll tell you about their novel they'll write someday. It's better than yours, it's perfect, because it doesn't really exist. It's a pretty little dream—a teenager's crush, a politician's promise, a magazine advertisement—perfection. But they haven't written it. Not a single word. Your messy, misshapen, novel-in-progress sitting at home still wins.

Existence beats perfection every time.

RAISE YOUR EXPECTATIONS

OWEN

I have a confession.

I haven't read *To Kill a Mockingbird*. Nor have I read *Middlemarch*, or even *Animal Farm*, nor all the novels of Faulkner or Hemingway or the Brontës.

I'm a novelist, a teacher of creative writing, a book reviewer, and I have yet to read some of the best novels of all time.

So many books, so little time. And I'm aware I won't get to them all before I'm six feet under. I won't even get to all the truly great ones.

This haunts me. This drives me.

We only get to read so many books in one lifetime. If someone chooses to read one of mine, they are sacrificing the opportunity to read another book. To be read is a huge gift. Readers are gifting me time and heart and head. I strive to honor that. I strive to give them something not just good, not just serviceable. I strive to give them something worth the sacrifice.

Honor the reader like a chef cooking for a king, crafting an exquisite meal. Honor the reader like a lover preparing a romantic rendezvous. I'm not aiming to be good. I'm going for great.

I may fail. But I'll fail brilliantly.

MAPS AND BACKROADS

Many writers, including us, map out where they hope the book will go—a chapter breakdown or a list of plot points or a basic outline. Like planning a road trip, you've made a schedule of highways you want to take and cities you hope to explore.

This helps, especially at the beginning of a trip. You're on the road, with a basic idea of where you're headed. And you type away with confidence, knowing GPS is there to guide you.

But don't be afraid to leave the highway and take a back road that doesn't even show up on the map. Don't be too careful. Don't be afraid to get lost. If you keep your eyes locked on the map, you'll miss the scenery.

Stephen King, in his memoir and craft companion *On Writing*, describes his technique for writing with the door closed and editing with the door open.

A closed door draft is a version of your manuscript that you will never show anyone. Never. It's a diary entry, a secret room, an internet search with no browser history. It's the lost weekend of drafts. You can be as wild, messy, uncomfortable, controversial as you want, because no one will ever read it. Abandon punctuation, write your deepest fears, try your hand at a bit of gore, be hateful, be sappy, it's all good. And even if it's bad, that's fine too. The words are only for you, and no one will see them.

Questions will arise. Keep writing. More often than not, the answer is hiding behind another thousand words.

You can pour out your book from start to finish, you can haphazardly throw down random chapters, or you can stream-of-conscious-write nonstop until you feel your tank is empty. The goal isn't to write a good book. The goal is to get out the almost-first draft of your book.

There's a secret waiting at the end of the last page. The book—or article or essay or story—has a secret it is waiting to whisper to you when you've typed that first messy, mangled draft. It will whisper what it hopes to be. You may have thought you were writing about the French Resistance in World War II, but the book may tell you, "You're writing about your father...again."

Listen to it! There's no wiser guide to your writing than your writing.

The trick is to plan your trip well, and leave room for inspired wandering. Get lost. It may be the perfect way to find your path.

At the end of the journey, you can return to the map. How far off course did you travel? Are you pleased with what you discovered? Have you ventured to that wonderful place in writing where no cartographer has visited, and the map simply reads, "Here be dragons"?

SURPRISE

No tears in the writer, no tears in the reader.
No surprise in the writer, no surprise in the reader.

Robert Frost

THE BOUNCER
IN MY BRAIN

Our seven-year-old loves asking us to make up a name of an animal that doesn't exist, something like an *orangashark* or a *poopapotamus*. Then, without missing a beat, he'll describe in great detail the physical attributes, dietary needs, and mating habits of the rare and deadly *poopapotamus*.

You ask your average adult to make up an encyclopedia entry for an as-yet-unheard-of creature and he'll sputter, cough, and say he can't think of anything.

Of course, that's a lie.

There're over eighty billion synapses firing across our brains every second. We are, quite literally, always thinking of something—billions of somethings.

So what's the difference between the seven-year-old and the thirty-seven-year-old?

Judgment.

Somewhere around the age of puberty we develop a sense of judgment. It's like a little bar bouncer in our brain gets tasked with patting down each thought to see if it's safe enough to be let out into the world. Most are not.

Judgment is not a bad thing. Our seven-year-old is much more apt to run naked through our yard—or a Target—than most adults. We adults are usually socially acceptable, thanks to the Bouncer in our brain saying, "Hey buddy, keep the pants on."

As writers we use judgment in editing and revising. It's an essential tool for sharpening sentences, condensing paragraphs, and focusing themes. Let the Bouncer kick your darlings to the curb.

But when we're facing that blank screen, we don't need the Bouncer slapping down every other idea. When we're judging each sentence as we write it, we're creating an unsafe space for ideas. An idea sees that Bouncer and stays the hell away. The idea hides out in the back of the brain and lets the safe, non-threatening, sure-to-please ideas cut to the front of the line.

But we want those ideas from the back of the brain. So we make a mental practice of giving the Bouncer the night off and opening the door wide. We don't just allow the ideas in, we welcome them with backslaps and cheers. And when word gets out that the gate is unwatched, ideas, memories, and images start strolling in. Including all those low-lifes the Bouncer kept out— the clichés, the wrong turns, and the clumsy sentences. It's a messy party, but memorable and unexpected things happen at messy parties. We don't care if the ideas are good or bad—that can be decided later—we want them all.

The silly ideas, the surprising ideas, the ones so immature or lust-driven or naïve or disturbing or even hateful that they would never dare step forward if the Bouncer were on duty. We need the dangerous ideas, the ones that scare us. The ones that sneak out at night when we're dreaming and make us fly or kill or screw with sweat-breaking verisimilitude.

Be grateful that for hours of the day those images and thoughts are kept at bay, allowing us to eat dinner with friends, drive kids to school, edit work. We don't need to be standing in the storm all day long, so appreciate the umbrella. But as a writer, you must be able to put that umbrella away and let the rain fall hard.

This is not the dismissal of craft. You've studied, you've read, you've developed your craft. Now stop thinking about it and write. Let all you've learned sink below the surface, and allow the unfiltered muck and life to float to the top. Craft is primarily control. But creation needs some chaos. It's the magic non-thinking of dance, improv, jazz, lovemaking, play.

Get alone with your page and invite the thoughts you won't let yourself think. Write with the freedom of knowing this draft need never be read.

Write like a drunk child. Humiliate yourself over and over. Scribble secrets you've never told anyone, scribble secrets you've never told yourself. Confess, lie, sing, babble, keep your fingers typing even when your words make no sense. Surprise your page, offend your page, amaze your page. Revel in the heat, the mess, the mistakes, and grin like a madman at the outright word-snap miracles coming to life.

Then press save.

Walk away.

You can revise tomorrow.

SURPRISE

How do you convince the Bouncer in your brain to take the night off?

One approach is to surprise yourself. Write into the unexpected. Want to teach your feet to dance? Shake the ground.

Here are a couple of games we play to help get our feet moving. For these exercises, you might pick something you're working on now, or you can choose a classic story to work with, like Goldilocks and the Three Bears, Oedipus Rex, or *Star Wars*.

LINE POP

This exercise is a classic improv game. To prep for it, you'll want to gather some slips of paper. Write on them some favorite song lyrics, some lines from books and movies. Go to your kitchen and write down phrases and sentences from packaged foods, from bottles of medicine, from cleaning solutions.

Set a timer for five minutes. Start writing. When your timer chimes, grab one of the slips of paper and read it—this line is the next line of your writing. Most likely, it makes no sense, so your job now is to weave it in contextually, and continue writing, with this new line adding to the flow of your narrative. Set another timer for three minutes. When it chimes, grab another line. Incorporate it into your text. Keep going.

A–Z

You can also distract your Bouncer. Give that inner editor something else to worry about.

For this improv game, each sentence you write will start with the next letter of the alphabet. So, the first sentence you write must start with a word that starts with A, then the second sentence B, then C, and so on. You don't need to start with A, though—you can start with the first letter of your name, you can choose a word and use those letters as the guide for your sentences.

This exercise gives that Type A internal editor something to worry about while you play. The Bouncer is so busy running through the alphabet, they forget to watch the door and all the wild ideas sneak in.

It also nudges your sentences in new directions. You're pushed out of your standard patterns and get to explore new syntax to meet the challenge.

DIGITS

357-1425
See that phone number? That's your writing challenge.

Your first sentence must have three words. Your next sentence, five words. Then a seven-word sentence. Then...gasp...a one-word sentence. Then four, two, and five.

This a great game to challenge your go-to rhythms, pushing you into a variety of sentence structures. Plus, the Bouncer is distracted with counting words, and the ideas run through into the party.

NEW CHOICE

Take a page of your writing, either something you've been working on or a new piece for this exercise. Now strike out your third, eighth, and final sentences. Rewrite them.

Do it again. Strike them out and rewrite them. Don't revise the sentences. Change them completely. Go in a different direction.

Another way of doing this same exercise is to set an alarm to go off every three minutes. Every time it rings, strike out the sentence you just wrote and write a completely different sentence. Don't write slowly here; pound it out. Throw those new choices down. Some will surprise you.

Don't worry about running dry. You've got enough creativity to fill an ocean.

GATHERING
FIREWOOD

The soul should always stand ajar.
Ready to welcome the ecstatic experience.

Emily Dickinson

FIRE

Let's start a fire.

Let's gather our memories, observations, and inventions like loose wood and set them burning, watch them transform into smoke and dancing licks of light that can warm a chill, illuminate the dark, or scar the skin.

Let's start a fire.

First, let's gather some wood…

MINDMAPS

Start with a word or phrase in the center of your page and circle it. It can be a word that relates to your project or a word picked at random. Draw some spokes coming out of your circled word, so it looks like a little sun in the middle of the page. At the end of each of these spokes write any words or phrases that you associate with the center word. *Noodle* might lead to *pasta* or *dinner* or *rhymes.* Now branch out from these words with more spokes and more words you associate with each of them.

As you create this word association mindmap, jump from word to word, writing quickly and following the threads and subconscious connections. Don't censor yourself. Don't edit. Say yes to every idea. Don't stop until you've got a page covered in ideas. See what words or images or ideas keep popping up.

Mindmaps stretch your creative muscles and allow less-than-obvious connections to rise to prominence. You can take words straight from the mindmap and use them to spark your writing. Choose three words and use them as the first phrase or title of a piece. Or find the word that's the farthest away conceptually from your initial word and use the two of them as prompts.

When focusing on a particular writing project, put your central idea or title in the center, and begin associating. You can branch out in any areas—characters, settings, plot points. Choose a character and explore everything from physical attributes to personality traits to how they interact with the other characters. Or start with a theme in your book you hope to wrestle with and follow the threads to images and ideas.

Some mindmaps will begin to center on a particular word, which inspires more spokes than any other. Other mindmaps spread out like the roots of an Aspen grove. Still others will look like a series of gears interacting.

The very picture will tell you plenty. Are there certain words or images that inspire you more than others? What words send out the most spokes? Notice what words come up repeatedly, which characters seem to have lots of information about them and which feel underdeveloped. You might discover whole themes that permeate the book that you hadn't realized yet.

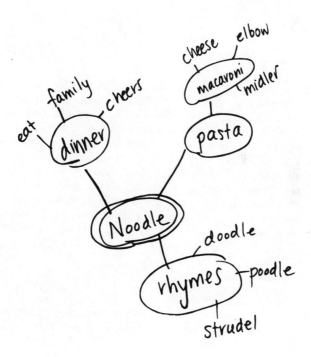

INSPIRATION JARS

WORD JARS

What to do with all those words that came from the mindmapping and brainstorming? First, gather up some jars—search in thrift stores, craft stores, or even tucked up in out-of-the-way kitchen cabinets. Choose jars you'd love to have sitting on your work surface. Then, print or write a slew of your mindmap words on slips of paper. You can put them all into one jar, or you can divide them up—by parts of speech (nouns, adjectives, verbs, full sentences), by mood (uplifting, calming, blue), by style (creepy, kid-friendly, sultry). Any time you want a boost, pluck out a word and throw it on the page. Every now and then, put your jars in a public part of your house along with some slips of paper and a pen, and let your family and friends add words to your jars.

IMAGE JARS

You can do the same with images—clippings from newspapers, pictures from the web, snapshots from your first year at summer camp, your honeymoon, your high school yearbook. For the personal essayist or memoirist, this can be an excellent way to harvest memories.

Collages make excellent brainstorming adventures. If you don't have a stack of old magazines, your nearby thrift store likely does. Or perhaps a stranger's high school yearbook. Thrift stores and estate sales are filled with photo albums of people you've never met. Each picture is just a story waiting to come to life.

Try making a collage portrait of your main characters. Or make a collage that captures the setting, the energy, the feel of your book. Explore a color and see where it takes you—use the collage as a brainstorming device, and see what sparks your interest. Watch what images draw your attention, and which you shy away from.

TREASURE JAR

Our kids are certified Thing Finders. They love picking up random treasures wherever they walk. Bits of metal, dismembered toy parts, smooth-edged rocks. Take yourself on a neighborhood stroll and keep your eyes peeled for tiny treasure objects. Keep them in a jar, and when the need strikes, pull one out, and use it as inspiration to launch your writing.

OWEN EGERTON · JODI EGERTON

EXERCISE

CLIPPINGS

MINDMAPPING WITH CLIPPINGS

Old magazines are a treasure trove for the writer seeking inspiration—choose a variety to capture different settings, different image styles, different writing styles. Use the images and words you clip from your stack of magazines as you mindmap. A child's face in an advertisement, one bold word stolen from a headline, half of a political cartoon. Let the map become a collage of ideas and images.

BLACKOUT POETRY

Choose a page from a magazine, a book, even some of your own writing. Using a black marker, circle words throughout the page to write a poem, a sentence, a story. Black out the other words, so you're left with just your chosen words on the page. This is a fun exercise, and is also a great reminder that we're all working with the same tools, the same words, and the most mundane magazine advertisement holds the ingredients for something spectacular.

RANSOM NOTE

Cut out words and phrases from a magazine and form a poem or story by arranging them on a page and gluing them down. The tactile experience of cutting the words, manipulating them, and gluing them uses different parts of your neural pathways than typing or handwriting words. Use this crafty exercise to release yourself when feeling stuck.

RANSOM NOTE EXTREME

Once again, cut words and phrases from a magazine and glue them down on a page. But this time, leave space between the words. Now go back and fill in words between the magazine cutouts. Your words mingle with the magazine words, and become something entirely new.

CUT-UP TECHNIQUE

Clipping and pasting can be more than just an exercise; it can be a means to an end. William S. Burroughs was famous for championing the cut-up technique, in which he would take a written page of his own work, cut it up into words and phrases, and randomly rearrange the pieces. David Bowie used a similar technique to craft some of his more outlandish lyrics.

PRAYER
SEX
PLAY

*Writing is like sex. First you do it for love, then you do it
for your friends, and then you do it for money.*

Virginia Woolf

WRITING AS PRAYER

The ritual, the quiet, the seriousness, the solitude. We pray onto the page.

At times prayer is begging, other times it is gushing gratitude, other times anger and questions and doubt. It can be wordless, but we writers love our words. Like David and Rumi, we are singing out prayers of faith, doubt, life—finding the words to voice the beating of our hearts. We carefully describe the world around us in wonder or disgust—we speak it.

Writing, like prayer, is reverent. In both, we ask our words to become something more than a symbol of meaning. Something mysterious. Our words become not only a tool of meaning but also a vessel for mystery.

WRITING AS SEX

Naked before the page.

We explore, touch, embrace. We surprise ourselves with sounds. We sweat. We forget everything but the room—then we forget even that. It is the words…and something just beyond the words.

It is intimate. Can sometimes be embarrassing. Often messy.

Even the most casual encounter can touch our hearts and change our lives.

It rewards the bold and excites the cautious and can be all kinds of fun.

WRITING AS PLAY

Make the rules, break the rules, laugh at the idea of any rules.
Skip from idea to idea.
Stop a game and begin again with no worries of regrets.
Risk and strive.

As you sit in a cardboard box in the backyard racing to save the universe from an alien horde, know that it's just a game *and* that the fate of all life on earth is at stake.

And don't even notice when the neighbors stare.

MUSIC

Some writers love having music in the background while they write; others need total silence. Some can only work with music without lyrics. We've found that we write to a lot of jazz—from Django Reinhardt to Charles Mingus—often focusing on one artist as the muse of a particular project. Owen also makes a mix that matches the tone of whatever he's working on. As he revises, he adds and subtracts from this playlist.

Explore the way music impacts your writing. Start by creating a playlist of five to ten songs, depending on how long you're able to devote to writing. Or program five radio stations that play a wide variety of music. Choose some slow songs and some fast songs, some instrumental and some with words. Some you know by heart and some you don't know at all.

As you write, allow the music to set the scene for you. Don't actively engage with the music, just let it be there, a companion as you write.

After your writing session finishes, take some time to assess—which songs helped propel you forward? Which distracted you? How does your writing adjust to the tempo and tone of the music playing?

QUESTIONS, GHOSTS, AND HIDDEN STONES

Ideas are like fish. If you want to catch little fish, you can stay in the shallow water. But if you want to catch the big fish, you've got to go deeper. Down deep, the fish are more powerful and more pure. They're huge and abstract. And they're very beautiful.

David Lynch

REAL BRIGHT HARD

We are miners, treasure hunters, deep sea divers. We spend these hours alone digging into our self, our memories, our expectations and prejudices, and prying out the stones we find. We carry our bright stones from the deepest caverns—often stumbling and blind—to the surface, to the light.

Writing is a sweet meeting of the private and public. We write in the private chambers of our soul, seeking emotions and truths we have perhaps never shared with our closest friends and family. Perhaps never shared with ourselves. Then we share this work—polished and clean—with the public, with strangers and enemies, and hopefully, the masses.

These hidden stones—soul stones and truth gems—do not have to be wild, new observations of the human spirit or a radical new approach to gender relations. They can be, of course. But they can be something simpler. Our souls—all our souls—are full of them. Born from the pressures and elements within, born from thinking and feeling through a lifetime. No need for radical experiences. Having a father was enough for Kafka. Having lived and felt. That's enough.

First taste of vomit.
Knowing you're going to die.
Understanding how very real the monster under the bed is.

Other stones surround us. Moments of humanity in all its shades.
A child watches his mother blush at the touch of his father.
A middle-aged man realizes he hates his son.
Two strangers on a bus make accidental eye contact as a mentally ill homeless person bellows.

Something of the earth. Something beautiful in the mud. Something real, bright, hard.

Carry it. Carry that moment, thought, feeling to the surface. Wash it and place it down for all to see. No need for too much stage lighting or too fancy a pillow. Just let it be there.

Real. Bright. Hard.

GHOSTS

Ghosts are fleeting and subtle, and all the more terrifying for it. Ghosts are sticky haunts, vague images of disturbing ideas. When a ghost skirts into view we generally turn away, click on the television, pour another drink until the light changes again and the phantom has passed on and we are left wondering if we saw anything at all.

But writers have a different calling.

Writers may fear ghosts, but we cannot afford to avoid them. We seek them. We choose to be haunted.

Break into haunted houses. Walk open-eyed through cemeteries. Call out to spirits and phantoms.

And when we encounter a feeble, inaudibly-crying specter, we don't run, we scribble. We sketch each ghastly detail, careful to read its mute lips as best we can, racing to capture the image, knowing how quickly a mist can dissipate, how easily a ghost can be spooked.

With each word we pen, the ghost gains flesh. Its eyes gleam, its lips thicken, the jaw begins to creak—bone on bone. We give it more, urging on the transformation. We strip our own skin, bit by bit, and lend it (we swear we're only lending it) to the ghost. Allowing it to form sinews, eyelids, a tongue.

Now speaking with our tongue, it begs for blood, promising no other words until the wish is granted. And we give it, gladly. We give with hours and thought and missteps and frustration and quiet contemplation and prolonged screams. We sew its skin and ask its name and wait for it to whisper why it is.

CIRCLE THE QUESTIONS

OWEN

My grandparents owned a loving, white-and-brown dog named Norman. He was my constant companion when we visited England in the summers. Running with us in the park, sitting loyally by my grandfather watching the BBC news, performing simple tricks for treats.

Back home in Texas, I came home from school one day to the news that Norman had been sick and the veterinarian had recommended putting him to sleep. My parents, both doctors, explained this was the kindest of courses. I was eleven, nearly twelve, and it confused my heart to think it was kinder to kill. What did this feel like for my grandparents? What did this feel like for Norman?

I went to my room, sick with questions. After some more tears, I sat at my desk and wrote. Without pre-thought, I began a story of Norman's last day. I wrote it from Norman's point of view—his physical pain and confusion, his recognition of my grandmother's sad face, his trust and comfort as my grandfather stroked his head and the vet administered the injection.

I sat at my desk writing in pencil until the sky waned dusk. Then I was done, the story complete—a simple, sentimental piece. There was nothing breathtakingly brilliant about the writing. But I felt better. I breathed easier. The writing had helped, but not in the way I had expected. I was no longer sick, but I had not answered a single one of my questions. Instead the story had given my questions and confusion a place to be.

I had written stories before—school room dramas, preadolescent romances, even a series of frantic adventures starring my own super-spy, Philip Duzmore. But Norman's story was a turning point. It was born from questions.

There are countless ways into a story or essay, but I'm drawn to the cracks made by questions. Questions that would be cheapened by answers. I am convinced that a life is defined more by the questions we return to than the answers we temporarily embrace. Those answers change, but we circle the questions again and again. Writing is how I circle the questions, examining the different sides, the contours and angles. Writing is my way into the questions where I can push outward, where I can be. I'm seeking something stranger than answers. As author Tim O'Brien says, "Fiction's purpose is not to explain the mystery, but to expand it."

There are plenty of writers who write from answers. They have discovered some truth and want to share it. Many of Tolstoy's stories, the later Walker Percy novels, and much of C.S. Lewis' prose fall into this category. These authors take me by the hand and offer to lead me somewhere. Sometimes that's exactly what I need. But I prefer the writers who are as lost as I am. Fyodor Dostoevsky, Annie Dillard, Scott Blackwood, Elie Wiesel. Writers who don't lead as much as allow me to join them on the search, who utter unanswerable questions, who expand the mystery.

REMEMBERING

Dig up a memory, one of those rough ones, that make you cringe when you think back on the situation.

First take some time to write it out—getting out a deeply-held memory can often release the most uncomfortable parts of the memory. Whenever we have a sticky situation in life, it swirls around in our brains until we release it by writing it down.

After you've gotten the whole story out, go back and rewrite it, but this time channel the memory through the perspective of someone else involved in the story. Remind yourself that this is all yours and no one else is going to read it.

What happens when you see that fight through the eyes of an onlooker? What if you get into the head of your archnemesis? What shifts, what cracks open? You might want to take a few rounds with this if you've got some strong negative feelings about the other person—write one round just focused on releasing all that negativity. And then write again and again from their perspective, from the outsiders' perspectives, trying to truly see the scenario from other points of view.

TURNING THE HANDLE

I love the entire process of converting research into fiction and think of it as composting. I try to toss rich, nutritious items onto the pile, horse manure, food scraps, along with grass clippings and dead leaves. I let it steep for months in a spot that receives ample sunshine. And I trust that a dark, buried world of microbial beings will convert the whole mass into a medium capable of sustaining a character, a story.

Sarah Bird

THE WAY IN

How does one enter into a story? What's the starting point for the narrative of a novel, personal essay, short story, or screenplay? We don't mean the first sentence; we mean the image or idea that leads the way into our writing. What's the way you turn the handle and open the door?

WORLD

Often, we find a world we want to explore. A prehistoric landscape in Jean M. Auel's *The Clan of the Cave Bear*, Eatonville in Zora Neale Hurston's *Their Eyes Were Watching God*, North Korea in Adam Johnson's *The Orphan Master's Son*.

Worlds can be as intriguing and influential as any character. Each world has its own rules, its own challenges, and even its own personality. A world can be as small as a corner of a stable, as in E.B. White's *Charlotte's Web*, or as expansive as a universe, as in Frank Herbert's *Dune* series. Don't mistake a smaller world for a smaller story. Tennessee Williams sets his plays, like *The Glass Menagerie*, almost exclusively in a small apartment. But the story looms large in human emotion. The writer must have a rich understanding of the world in which her characters live. This includes the scaffolding—does gravity exist? Is magic possible? Are all endings happy? But also deeper questions—what's at stake? Does justice exist? Can horrible things happen to our characters? Even if the characters don't discover the deep workings of their environment, the writer must have a clue as to how the world works.

Once you've been drawn to a world, you can craft the best character to explore that world. When writing *The Hobbit*, J.R.R. Tolkien chose a hero who was as unaware of Middle Earth outside the Shire as we were. So along the journey, Bilbo studies the world with curiosity and voices our own questions in a way that a more seasoned traveler of Middle Earth never would. To make it even better, Bilbo is not all that sure he wants to be on this trip. In protest, he bounces against the walls of the world and, by doing so, illuminates the world for the reader.

CHARACTER

Sometimes your way into the story is a character. John Kennedy Toole's Ignatius J. Reilly in *A Confederacy of Dunces*, Holden Caulfield in *The Catcher in the Rye* by J.D. Salinger, or Beverly Cleary's Ramona Quimby.

Don't make the mistake of thinking that your characters need to be perfect or worse, likeable. Celebrate their flaws. Explore their idiosyncrasies. Revel in their mistakes. Leo Tolstoy's Anna Karenina is an unrepentant adulteress. Jeff Lindsay's Dexter is an insatiable serial killer. These characters are better than likeable—they're intriguing. And we find them intriguing not in spite of their flaws, but in part *because* of their flaws.

One of the wild gifts of reading is empathizing with a character who is radically different from ourselves. Whether it's the memoir of a racist or the fictional exploits of a diamond thief, we recognize in them the same emotions and same character traits that we see in our own lives. The only real unforgivable crime that your central character can commit is being boring.

Memorable characters are more often than not active characters, individuals who reach out and interact negatively or positively with the world and people around them. They have goals and desires that drive them forward. If a character is passive, the story often focuses on how this character is pushed into action. Storytelling is rich with reluctant heroes, from *The Odyssey*'s Odysseus to *Star Wars: The Force Awakens*' Rey. But these characters are soon pushed past their resistance into action.

Entering into a story through a character can guide you in creating the other story elements.

When you have a particular character bursting onto the page, you must craft a world that will highlight all the intricacies of your hero.

Mark Twain knew the character of Huckleberry Finn from his childhood. As he writes in his autobiography, "In Huckleberry Finn I have drawn Tom Blankenship exactly as he was. He was ignorant, unwashed, insufficiently fed; but he had as good a heart as ever any boy had."

What world and adventure can best highlight Huck's freedom? Twain chooses a river journey that allows for episodic adventures. From town to town we get to see the folk-wise boy bounce up against bigots, con artists, slave hunters, and feuding families. Huck's own wisdom and transparently kind heart are all the more clear as he interacts with devious adults claiming wisdom. And much of the humor of the novel is found when it puts the fiercely independent Huck in compromising positions. Twain has this dirty, shoeless, wild child, and he puts him in a dress having tea and helping a housewife knit.

Place an active character in a challenging world, and you can't help but discover story.

QUESTION

Many writers enter into a narrative with a question. The screenplay for *Back to the Future* (Robert Zemeckis, Bob Gale) began when Bob Gale wondered what it would be like to have met his dad as a teenager. In *Pet Sematary*, Stephen King asks if we'd bring back the dead, no matter the cost. The questions that hide deep, the ones that have no firm answer, make for compelling writing.

Nora Ephron's screenplay *When Harry Met Sally* is based on the question: Can a man and a woman be friends? It's possible to watch the entire film as an investigation into that question.

A question that has an easy answer makes a weak entrance into a story. If you enter into a piece of writing with the question "Is it wrong to hurt children," you'll find you have a thin piece of propaganda. Ask questions for which you don't yet know the answer.

JOURNEY

Point A to point B can be a beautiful and useful scaffolding for a story—fiction or nonfiction. It can be a physical journey like John Steinbeck's *The Grapes of Wrath*. Or a rags-to-riches journey like Charles Dickens' *Great Expectations*. Or a journey from one state of being to another like Mary

Karr's *Lit*.

The journey provides a pacing complete with mile markers and finish lines. Often the route is marked out in the early stages of a story. The surprises come from the unexpected obstacles, alternative routes, and personal arc. Cheryl Strayed's *Wild* would be nothing more than a hiker's travelogue if it weren't for her paralleled internal journey dealing with addiction, relationships, and self-discovery.

MOMENT

Sometimes one moment is all you need to enter a piece. Often an essayist will focus on a moment of change or discovery and build their essay around it, examining how the time, world, and history influenced the moment. Corbyn Hanson Hightower chose an off-the-cuff comment from her husband and crafted around it the hilarious and heart-wrenching essay, "My Husband Had a Vasectomy and All I Got Was This Lousy T-Shirt."

A moment can also be the way in to longer works. The momentum of Kerouac's *Big Sur* is found in the promise of a coming moment—the hour he goes "mad." The moment can be less extraordinary. Faulkner related that the genesis of his novel *The Sound and the Fury* was peeking into a window and falling back into a mud puddle. From that one moment, he discovered his masterpiece.

An image, a phrase, and a passing glance can all be the speck around which a pearl is formed.

OLD STORY, NEW TWIST

You can take any story and change up an element of it, and you'll have a whole new story to explore. This can be as simple as a change of location. Imagine *Wuthering Heights* taking place in an arctic science lab. Or it can be a more personal change. What if Lancelot had fallen in love not with Guinevere but with Arthur?

It can also be a twist on point of view. *Wicked* tells the story of the *Wizard of Oz* from the perspective of the Wicked Witch of the West. It's a story we already know, but seen from a fresh angle. An old story is made new.

In the Tom Stoppard play *Rosencrantz and Guildenstern Are Dead*, it's a shift of focus that breathes life into a known story. In the play we follow the stories of two minor characters from Shakespeare's *Hamlet*. The traditional story of the Danish prince becomes merely background for a startlingly moving drama.

FAN FICTION

E. L. James made news with her *Fifty Shades of Gray* series, which began as *Twilight* fan fiction. In fan fiction, you take a known story as your launching point and then take the characters on new adventures. Writing fan fiction is a great exercise for fiction writers, as the characters are already developed, and the settings and plotlines often are as well. You'll focus your work on writing dialogue, narrative arc, and crafting crisp clean sentences. Your readers will call you out if you don't draw the characters or their reactions believably.

It can also be intoxicatingly fun to place beloved characters in unexpected, even erotic, situations.

MIXING IT ALL UP

Stephen Sondheim's *Into the Woods* combines classic characters from fairy tales (Rapunzel, Cinderella, Prince Charming, Red Riding Hood), with newly crafted characters, and throws them all into a brand new plotline. Audiences don't need much to understand Cinderella—they know her story—so Sondheim has the freedom to play around with the audience's expectations. We see Cinderella running away from the ball, but then see her trying to avoid the prince, not interested in marrying him. Take a story we know and give us a tangled up version of it.

MAKE IT MODERN

A Christmas Carol is a prime example of a story we see reenergized often with new actors, new settings, new visions. Disney scored a major hit with

The Little Mermaid, a story plucked from a Hans Christian Anderson fairy tale but re-visioned within the Disney formula and transformed into a musical with a happy ending. In *The Carriage House*, Louisa Hall reimagined *Little Women* and set it in 21st century America. And, of course, countless theater companies and film directors have reimagined a Shakespearian play in a modern setting.

Don't be afraid to reimagine a classic story in a different setting. Not only will it squeeze fresh revelations out of a known tale, often it will lead to a completely new story.

MIX AND MATCH

List six books or movies you love. Beside them list their genres. Now try mixing and matching.

What if *Jaws* were a comedy?

What if *Jane Eyre* were sci-fi?

List six books or films and note some of the characters, minor and major. Now play with the story from new points of view.

What if *Alien* were seen from the point of view of the alien?

How would Daisy tell the story of *The Great Gatsby*? How would Tom tell it?

BUG OFF

This is an exercise in moving outwards from reality toward the more fantastical. Here's how it goes:

First, pick a critter that bugs you. In our house, it'd be fruit flies, giant roaches, lice, or fire ants. Write for fifteen minutes inspired by those critters. You might write about how much you hate them. You might describe the moment when you see your kid scratch her hair and you know the lice are back. You might word-associate around the feeling of a mosquito bite itching.

Second, write for another fifteen minutes watching and describing the critter itself. Get down there with a microscope or a zoom lens and pretend you're a nature documentarian.

And third, take that same critter and now write for fifteen minutes from their perspective. First person, their voice, their reactions, their experiences.

MUSEUM DISCOVERY

Go to a museum and hit a section you usually ignore.

You might go to a local museum, or find a statue in a park, a mural on the side of a school. If you don't have access to any of these, you can even search online through museum websites.

Find a work of art that interests you. Sit with it. Push yourself to stay a little longer than feels like enough. Make yourself center with it, present, open. Look at the lines, the brushstrokes, the materials. Try to find some aspect of it that you don't ordinarily notice in art.

While still present with the work of art, write for about fifteen minutes. Write what you see, write what you feel, write where your mind goes. Try to capture the visual in words.

Later, give yourself another writing session. This time, take the energy and feeling of your experience with the work of art, and use that to launch your writing. The challenge this time, though—you can write about other subject, but not the work of art itself.

GENRE TOURISM

An essential part of writing is reading. In this exercise, challenge yourself to read something from a genre you usually avoid. Romance, science fiction, mystery, thriller, poetry, creative nonfiction. If you're usually into *New York Times* best sellers, pick up that classic you've never read. If you're proud of your Ph.D. program reading list, find a mass market paperback, some good pulp fiction.

This is also an exercise you can practice with a friend. Each of you gets to give the other a blind date book, wrapped in paper, both agreeing to read the book no matter what's underneath the wrapping.

FIRESTARTERS

I'm a complete cynic in every part of my life except writing—a novel coming together is absolute magic and a gift. I just try to make my brain ready, give it details and slow-smoked brisket and hope for the best.

Amanda Eyre Ward

LIGHTING THE FIRE

So we gather our characters, our settings, and our themes like firewood. But without a spark, it's just a stack of dead wood.

Where the hell do we find a spark?

LIGHTNING

Fire falls out of the sky. A slash of white light snaps from the clouds and hits the earth like a gift from the gods. Sometimes inspiration hits us like lightning. We are shocked by an idea that seemed to come out of nowhere. It's enough to set our writing ablaze.

Plenty of writers wait for inspiration to strike.

And wait.

And wait.

Don't wait for lightning. Hunt down thunderstorms.

Writing is more than sitting in front of a blank page. It is living an internal and external life that invites electricity.

Seek out the parts of town people avoid. Take a job at a mortuary. Look up heartsick stories in the back of vintage newspapers.

Follow questions like storm clouds.

Could I have been a Nazi?

What are the borders of my love for my spouse?

If God asked me to commit an act of violence against someone I loved, would I follow?

This can lead to some dark nights, but what better place to witness a thunderstorm.

What are the dreams I have for my children?

What does perfect love look like?

What would it feel like to reach enlightenment?

Now watch where the lightning hits the ground, run there and gather the fire.

BORROW A SPARK

Fire can be found all around you.

It can be a line of poetry, an overheard strand of gossip, a sentiment shared by a loved one. Sometimes these flames are brief, lasting but a moment. But if we're quick, we catch their fire and use it to light our own.

Don't mistake inspiration for thievery. Ever light a candle from another candle? The first candle burns just as brightly. The flame isn't stolen. Fire tends to spread.

So go to your favorite poets, songwriters, photographers, and beg for a spark. Keep your ears open in public places, and around children at play.

Take that spark and build your fire.

LIGHTER FLUID

Sometimes the words don't burn. You've got your characters, you've got your setting, but something's not working. Perhaps what you need is a little lighter fluid.

Lighter fluid is an added element that helps a blaze begin. It can be a revealed secret, a ticking clock, even an annoying fly buzzing around a character's ear. Remember, lighter fluid helps *start* a fire, but without characters and story—without something that burns—it's just a flash.

Lighter fluid can be simple. A man is trying to pick a lock on his ex-wife's safe. She's downstairs entertaining guests. He has only a few minutes. Already this is pretty good. Now add a splash of lighter fluid. The man has to pee. Desperately.

Be warned: too much lighter fluid can overwhelm what you really want to burn. A man is about to ask his beloved for her hand in marriage. To increase the drama, you add a fleet of alien spaceships descending upon the Earth. That's a lot of lighter fluid. And your original story of the young couple is lost in the flash.

But in the right amount, an added distraction, an outside pressure, or a piece of new information can set your scene on fire.

MAGNIFY

Ever use a magnifying glass to squeeze some sun into a burning beam of light? You can blister skin, torture an ant, or start a brush fire. This same technique can aid your writing.

Take an object, a moment, a memory, or a single word and look at it—not a passing glance, but an intense examination. We become the magnifying glass, our gaze becomes the focused light. Our subject shares its secrets and scars.

Essayist and novelist Annie Dillard is a master at moving ever closer to a subject until the intensity of her gaze sets the subject ablaze. She'll watch a single water beetle for hours, ponder a hundred-year-old diary reference to clouds, examine a personal fear well past the point most of us would turn away. One element becomes an entry point to discovery and beauty.

This approach takes patience and presence. If you want to see a bud bloom, you're going to have to be there, quiet and open-eyed. Move close enough to hear its whispers, and stay long enough to witness its petals unfold.

TWO STICKS

The time-proven method of finding a spark and starting a fire is the simple action of rubbing two sticks together. Take two solid characters, ideas, expectations, or goals and let them collide. Let them smack against each other again and again.

It's possible to have a story without conflict. Science writer and jellyfish aficionado Juli Berwald turned us on to the ancient Eastern conflict-free narrative structure of Kishōtenketsu. And Robert Boswell has experimented with stories of transformation and life changes that avoid outright conflict. But most of our stories rely on the heat of tension caused by clashing forces or ideas or personalities.

We both served as artistic directors for the National Comedy Theater in Austin, Texas, for some years. We taught that a simple way to find the story in an improvised scene is to find the clash of values. Take two people who have opposing desires and stick them in a room together.

This can be as simple as a Bert and Ernie sketch on *Sesame Street*. Bert wants to sleep. Ernie eats cookies noisily. Bert covers his head with a pillow. Ernie starts practicing his trumpet. The more Bert wants to sleep, the more frantically he begs for silence, the more satisfying it is as Ernie gleefully makes more of a racket. The more the desires clash, the more energy the story has. The tension escalates and a story catches fire.

Monty Python are experts at this kind of scene building. A customer wants cheese. The clerk at the cheese shop has no cheese. A man believes a parrot is dead. His counterpart tries to convince him it is alive.

Simple as two sticks rubbing together.

The power comes in the conflict.

If Ernie had also wanted to sleep or if Bert was up to listen to Ernie's music, the tension would be erased. We'd have two sticks laying side by side and no chance at a fire.

Watch an orchestra. Watch the musician play the cymbals. She takes two cymbals and attempts to have them occupy the same space at the same moment. The result is a clash brilliant enough to punctuate a symphony.

WILDFIRES

It's getting dark. It's already cold. The kids are moaning, gripping an already-opened bag of marshmallows. And you can't seem to get that damn fire going. You've stacked the wood perfectly, gathered kindling, kept the matches dry. Every attempt begins promisingly enough. A few orange-red flickers, an excited cheer from the kids, and you carefully guide the fire to life. But soon enough the flames die and you're left with nothing but smoke wisps and raw s'mores.

And yet forest fires are accidentally set thousands of times a year. What are they doing by accident that you can't do on purpose?

Truth is, fire needs freedom. Fire wants to reach beyond the boundaries you've set, it wants to burn wildly, out of control, finding fuel in the underbrush and treetops.

Often you need no other fire starter than the freedom to let the flames burn. There's a time for control and craft. There's also a time to let the writing burn like a forest fire.

IN THE BEGINNING...

Writing is a kind of ongoing struggle to renew the world.

Karl Ove Knausgaard

WARNING

OWEN

Through much of the rest of the book, we'll be discussing story structure, but first a warning. While studying for my MFA at Texas State University—a program I thoroughly enjoyed—I completed a strange, dark story that I was very happy with. I brought it to one of my instructors, an accomplished and talented writer. He told me the structure was flawed and the story failed. He recommended I rework or abandon it.

He was right. The structure was bizarre. I was tempted to take his advice and rework the story or throw it out. But here's the thing—I dug the story. Something about it was working, even if it *shouldn't* have worked.

Wonderful things happen when you disobey the rules. The rhythmless radicalness of Walt Whitman, the pistol-whip speed of Lydia Davis, the fever dream logic of James Reich and Ben Marcus.

Craft lessons and how-to books can be wonderful. They can guide the shape of your story, help you clarify the beats and rhythm of your work, but they can also be a soul-squelching wet blanket of boredom. That includes this book. Be wary of anyone telling you how to write. It's all too close to a how-to sex guide. Read all you want, then make your own way.

By the way, I didn't change that story of mine. The story was published, I later adapted it into a screenplay, and it became the first feature I directed. All that to say, structure is important, but it's not all-important.

BEGINNINGS

You begin with the world working. A certain kind of balance has been achieved. It can be a happy family, a peaceful town, a gleeful single woman. Or perhaps it's not a healthy balance. Perhaps a couple remains married because of the unwritten rule to never speak of the husband's multiple affairs. They're married, just not *happily* married. Or cops turn a blind eye to local mobsters as long as they get their slice of the pie. The system is corrupt, but operating.

The writer's job is to stop it from working. Toss a wrench into the machinery. Throw the character or world out of balance. A monster arrives in the peaceful town, the single woman meets a person she can't live without, the grown offspring of one of the husband's affairs knocks on the front door. Suddenly the part that kept the engine running snaps. The story begins when what a world or person does to survive no longer works.

This initial shift in balance goes by many names. We like the term Inciting Incident.

CALL TO ACTION

Often the Inciting Incident comes in the form of a Call to Action. A character is urged to partake in a journey or challenge and the adventure of the story presents itself. Gandalf arrives at Bilbo's house, a letter addressed to Harry Potter slides through the mail slot at #4 Privet Drive, Hamlet is charged by the ghost of his father to avenge his death.

Usually this Call to Action is initially resisted. The character denies the call and clings to the balance of their lives. But the action of the story soon propels them into the adventure.

As Joseph Campbell has pointed out, Homer's *The Odyssey* offers a classic example of the Call to Action. The heroic Odysseus is urged to leave his wife and son and join the war in Troy. But he's happy at home. The Call throws his life out of balance. One could read all of *The Odyssey* as the hero's struggle to reestablish the original balance. After some prodding from the gods, Odysseus goes to war, performs his duty, and then faces the decade-long journey to reach home and return to domestic life.

The same Call to Action surprises Luke Skywalker in George Lucas' *Star Wars: A New Hope*. Luke finds a holographic distress message from Princess Leia—his invitation to adventure. But in this tale, Luke has no desire to return to his Tatooine moisture farm. Instead he yearns for a new balance and a secret wisdom.

Stories with happy endings move from balance to balance lost and finally to a new, wiser balance.

UNAVOIDABLE ACTION

Sometimes the Inciting Incident is not so much a Call to Action as it is action being thrust upon a character. A novelist is rescued/kidnapped by a psychotic fan in Stephen King's *Misery*. A wandering sailor is shipwrecked in Daniel Defoe's *Robinson Crusoe*. In these situations, the characters have no choice but to confront their newly unbalanced world. They may initially choose despair over action, but will eventually work toward establishing some kind of new balance.

NEW IDENTITY

Another way to push a character off balance is to thrust a new identity upon them. A character facing a new identity must stumble in shoes that don't yet fit across an unfamiliar terrain. The dance toward balance helps drive the narrative. A woman discovers she's a werewolf or, as in Mark Twain's *The Prince and the Pauper*, a poor boy finds himself in the lap of luxury while his royal doppelgänger experiences the life of an impoverished citizen. Harry Potter receives his Call to Action *and* the revelation of his true identity on the same day. The effect is dizzying.

In stories of mistaken identity, as in *Moulin Rouge!* (Baz Luhrmann, Craig Pearce) or *North by Northwest* (Ernest Lehman), a character's balanced life is interrupted by accident. Often in these cases, the hero will begin by trying to correct the mistake and reclaim their own identity. But usually they end up embracing the adventure and discovering an altogether fresh identity shaped by their experiences. Again, the goal of returning to the original balance is abandoned for a new, more intriguing balance.

BEST/WORST

One of the most effective ways to craft an Inciting Incident is to imagine the best or the worst thing happening to your character. In the opening chapters of Donna Tartt's *The Goldfinch*, we follow a mother and son just long enough to understand their mutual love. The mother is the most important person in the boy's life. Then a bomb explodes, killing the mother and orphaning the son. It is the worst thing possible in his world.

As the noble war hero Macbeth returns from battle, three witches predict he will be the next king of Scotland. It's the best thing.

Occasionally the Inciting Incident is simultaneously the best *and* the worst thing that could happen. In James Cameron's *Titanic*, Jack wins tickets on a luxury cruise back home to America—the best! But of course the boat is the doomed Titanic—the worst! Romeo meets Juliet. It's love at first sight—the best! But she's the one person he's forbidden to love—the worst. Or in *Casablanca* (Julius and Philip Epstein), Ilsa walking into Sam's bar is the Inciting Incident. She's the one woman Sam has ever loved, but she also broke his heart. Seeing her again is both his deepest desire and worst fear. The best and the worst.

Pixar Studios are masters at shaping Inciting Incidents in the first ten minutes of their feature films. In *Up* (Bob Peterson, Pete Docter) we watch a lifelong love affair end with the death of our hero's wife—the worst. In *Cars* (Dan Fogelman, John Lasseter, Joe Ranft, Kiel Murray, Phil Lorin, Jorgen Klubien) Lightning McQueen wins the chance to compete for the highest honor in racing and achieve his dream—the best. In Brad Bird's *The Incredibles*, Mr. Incredible and Elastigirl get married just as superheroes are made illegal—the best and the worst.

These moments throw the character off balance and provide the seeds that the rest of the story grows from. How our character responds to the pressure of the best/worst event informs the entire narrative.

Consider *Finding Nemo* (Andrew Stanton, Bob Peterson, David Reynolds). In the opening minutes of the film, our hero, Marlin, loses his wife and all but one unhatched egg to a hungry eel. It's the worst thing possible. Marlin has a choice of how to respond to this event—basically the balanced reaction or the unbalanced reaction. Nearly always the hero chooses the unbalanced response. Marlin becomes an overprotective, if doting, father to his one surviving child. We recognize he's being overprotective, but because we witnessed the Inciting Incident, we forgive him. It's understandable the guy is a little hyper-concerned; he lost almost his entire family to an eel!

A nervous Marlin finally allows Nemo to join the other young aquatic life at school. But when he learns the class is heading to the reef drop-off, Marlin overreacts. He rushes to Nemo and orders him back home. Marlin's unbalanced parenting drives Nemo to rebel and swim off the reef where he is captured by a scuba diver and carried away. Marlin rushes after him and spends the majority of the film finding Nemo.

If Marlin had a balanced response to the loss of the initial eel attack and not become an overprotective parent, Nemo would not have been pushed to rebel, would not have been caught, and we'd not have had a story. Instead, Marlin's unbalanced reaction to the Inciting Incident propels the characters into the major action of the story.

Finding his son is our hero's clear surface goal. But equally important to the narrative is Marlin's journey toward balance. During his quest he'll discover risk and fun are as essential to parenting as protection. In fact, he'll be more worldly and adventurous than he was even in the film's opening moments.

Our hero begins with balance. In the Inciting Incident she is toppled off-balance. She seeks to reestablish balance, but during the course of the story discovers a new and more fulfilling balance.

THE LOGIC OF DREAMS AND NIGHTMARES

DREAMS DON'T MAKE SENSE.

The dead walk. The ground melts. The pigeons all sing, "Hey Jude." Images flow into images and we move among them with no resistance. The intensity of our emotions wavers inappropriately so that in our sleep we weep over a broken pencil and feel nothing for a dying child.

In dreams we discover flight and wild power. We meet our heroes and seduce long-lost lovers. In dreams we're guilty of murder and hate. In dreams we drown and fall.

DREAMS DO MAKE SENSE.

The laws of physics, the workings of time, and the appearance of reality all twist, but there is sense all its own. We *feel* it. The impossible flying thrills us just the same. The inexplicable public nudity shames us nonetheless. The implausible cannot be dismissed. Math is useless in dreams.

The structures and formats we study are lost in dreams. Instead a new, deeper thinking bubbles to the surface. It's dream logic. Fantastical sense. Nightmare swimming.

The wonderful truth is, we relate to the strangest dreams. We hear another's nightmare and understand the terror, even if the nightmare is set in an illogical world. Gabriel García Márquez's magical realism, the strangescapes of Franz Kafka, the hilarious and haunting absurdities of Amelia Gray. We understand the images and arcs in a place below rational thought. A primitive, soul-rich place. A place of dreams.

As we dream onto the page, sometimes we must abandon the rules of reality and understanding of causation. These are times to celebrate dream logic, explore nightmare thinking, and fly through a world with eyes wide open.

TORTURE YOUR
CHARACTER

*Be a sadist. No matter how sweet and innocent your
leading characters, make awful things happen to them—
in order that the reader may see what they are made of.*

Kurt Vonnegut

OBSTACLES THAT DEMAND ACTION

How do we know Romeo loves Juliet? Their words? The things the two have in common? The soft eyes they make at one another? Not quite. Romeo and Juliet's love story, and most every love story that follows, is centered not on what brings the couple together, but on what keeps them apart. The key to great love stories is the obstacles that inspire action.

We understand the intensity of Juliet and Romeo's love by witnessing the obstacles they are willing to overcome to be with one another. You could argue that the two teenagers themselves would never have discovered the value of their love had it not been for the high price they were pushed to pay.

If these two kids are neighbors whose parents get along just fine, we'd have no story no matter how much they love each other. They'd just be another happy Italian couple in passionate love. Or maybe not so passionate—perhaps their love rose to meet the obstacles.

Obstacles necessitate action, and action defines character. We know a character not by what they say or think, but by what they do. As Aristotle puts it: "All human happiness and misery take the form of action."

Our job as writers is to torture our characters.

Create a character. Give her a dream, a desire so deep it defines her. Give her the courage to pursue that dream. And throw everything you can in her way. Try your best to stop her and watch her either rise to the occasion or crumble.

Put hell itself in the way. That's what Mark Twain did.

How much does Huck Finn love Jim? The two have plenty of adventures. But it's not until Huck sets forth to rescue Jim from slavery, believing the act will damn his soul to hell, that we—and he—understand his devotion to the man.

You will never know how strong a character is until you give her an obstacle to prove it. Put a wall up in front of your character and watch as she learns she can knock it down.

Don't worry about going too far—you can always pull back later. Challenge your character and yourself to face the most difficult of obstacles.

Think about that beautiful literary masterpiece *Die Hard*, penned by screenwriters Steven E. de Souza and Jeb Stuart adapting a Roderick Thorp novel. The writers work ceaselessly to make John McClane's adventure as difficult as possible. Make him outnumbered, put him in unknown territory, beat him to a pulp. They take away his shoes. And then they scatter broken glass on the floor. I'm sure, more than once, the writers stopped and thought, "Oh crap. I've gone too far. How do I get him out of this one?"

But the writers and John McClane live up to the challenge—something that is impossible to do if the challenge isn't there.

Our job as writers is to put our characters through the wringer. Make them hurt. Challenge their values. Put them in impossible situations. Paint them into a corner so they have to learn to fly.

There's a wonderful moment in Brad Bird's *The Incredibles* when Dash, the speedy young superhero, is being chased by the bad guys. He's running for his life, facing huge obstacles. He breaks through the jungle foliage and finds a lagoon. Instead of sinking, as he expected, he looks down and finds he's running fast enough to run on water. He chuckles with delight and speeds on.

Dash never would have known he had the ability to run on water if it hadn't been for the dangers and challenges he was facing. Plot, at its simplest level, is a series of obstacles which demand action that reveals character.

THAT FISH CAN'T BREATHE

You walk into an unknown dark room. How do you explore the space? You move to the walls, you feel out where the corners are, you touch the boundaries. If you know the room, you can most likely walk through it even in the dark. There's no need to explore its shape.

Take a world—the circus, the drug market, the jungle—and create the least likely person to be in that place. Put a character who will bounce against the walls and they will let the reader know where the walls are. The character's friction with their surroundings will power the story. A character perfectly at home in a situation or place provides no questions, no tension, no fuel for the narrative. But a character in conflict is story.

How do we explore the bizarre world of beauty pageants? We could follow an aspiring beauty queen through a contest, but she's going to walk straight through that dark room, never reaching for the walls. Instead, let's create a character who's crude, clumsy, and a stranger to high heels and eyeliner. We'll make her an undercover FBI agent who's more at home at a shooting range than a photo shoot. This gives us *Miss Congeniality* (Marc Lawrence, Katie Ford, Caryn Lucas).

The fish-out-of-water predicament is a classic source of comedy. The pauper changes places with the prince, the pampered rich girl finds herself in basic training, hillbillies hit Beverly Hills—characters spiral into a world they don't get. The reader or viewer learns the rules of this world by witnessing the character breaking the rules. The character doesn't just feel out the walls in the dark room, she slams into them, bouncing from wall to wall like a pinball.

But a fish out-of-water situation is not always funny. In creating *Breaking Bad*, Vince Gilligan intentionally crafted the least likely character to become a bloodthirsty drug lord—a nebbishy high school chemistry teacher—and pushed him into the world of meth dealing. In Edna Ferber's novel *Giant*, an East Coast socialite finds herself in the foreign land of a west Texas ranch. Harrison Ford plays a city cop going undercover as an Amish farmer in *Witness* (Earl W. Wallace, William Kelley). The characters step over every line, break the unwritten rules, and map out the territory for the audience or reader. The characters continue to find their expectations and values in a clash with the expectations and values of their new world. That tension heats the story.

The struggle can be more than just a series of failures to fit in. Sometimes it's a character in open conflict with an institution or system. Holden Caulfield in J.D. Salinger's *Catcher in the Rye*, Jude Fawley in Thomas Hardy's *Jude the Obscure*, and Captain John Yossarian in Joseph Heller's *Catch 22* are excellent examples. The characters stand in opposition to the culture or system in which they find themselves.

A more subtle twist on the theme of fish-out-of-water is when the water is still there, but the fish can no longer breathe. Think of Franz Kafka's Gregor Samsa in *The Metamorphosis* waking up to find himself transformed into a large bug. The world has not changed, but he is now the alien in what was once his home.

Allow your worlds to challenge, annoy, and even terrify your characters. Let them struggle against the reality in which they find themselves. There's a story in every flopping fish—a struggle, a goal, a spark. A fish swimming along in a perfectly safe coral reef is the stuff of screen savers, not stories.

ODD COUPLING

Mortal enemies. Buddy cops. Mismatched lovers. When opposing characters are forced together through circumstance, goals, or love, then narratives ensue.

Memoirist and novelist Debra Monroe once remarked that in our lives, most of us try to avoid conflict, but in our writing we have to lock enemies in the same room.

Felix likes things clean and organized. Oscar likes a mess and a few cigars. In the *Odd Couple*, Neil Simon took two opposites and forced them into a room together. The two push each other's buttons and a story is born. In his memoir *A Walk in the Woods*, Bill Bryson is joined on his hike along the Appalachian Trail by his brash, physically unfit friend Stephen Katz. Though the descriptions of the mountains and forests are wonderful, it is this unlikely pairing that works as the heart of the story. The same can be said for nearly every buddy-cop movie from *48 Hours* (Roger Spottiswoode, Walter Hill, Larry Gross, Steven E. de Souza) to *The Heat* (Katie Dippold).

This doesn't have to be mutual antagonism. In *Planes, Trains and Automobiles*, Steve Martin's Neal Page grows more desperate to abandon John Candy's Del Griffith. But Del is more than happy to buddy up with Neal. Writer/director John Hughes finds great comic fuel in this added clash of desires. It's just one more thing these two disagree about.

Once you've got two characters who would never choose to be in the same room, your job is to shove them in a broom closet. Find the shared goal, need, or compulsion that drives these two together. The chief has demanded they work together; they both have to get to the other side of the country by Thanksgiving, and there's only one rental car available; someone has handcuffed the two together. The force that compels them to share a space or journey must be equal to or greater than the desire to get the hell away from one another. As the force driving them apart increases, the forces keeping them together must match it. Otherwise you'll have your reader or viewer muttering, "Why doesn't he just ditch that guy?"

What Neal discovers in *Planes, Trains and Automobiles*, as do so many of these characters, is that the person they don't *want* is the person they *need* in some way. The one provides a skill or emotional element lacking in the other. They complete each other.

This is why odd coupling works so well in romance stories. Love provides both the shared goal that forces the unlikely pair together and the reward for sticking it out. It's a sitcom trope now to have a couple simultaneously driven together and driven apart. In *Cheers* (created by James Burrows, Glen Charles, Les Charles) Sam and Diane are perfectly mismatched and rub each other the wrong way at every turn. That's what makes them a fun, story-driving couple. To paraphrase Tolstoy, happy couples are dull as hell.

If having a shared goal can bring characters together, so can pursuing diametrically opposed goals. One person wants to get the ball across the line, the other wants to stop him. In Victor Hugo's *Les Misérables*, Jean Valjean desires freedom and Inspector Javert is dedicated to capturing him. The two are actively and thematically in opposition. Valjean manages amazing escapes inspired by the relentless pursuit of Javert. In a sense, the one brings out the best in the other. And Hugo does a brilliant job of having the two organically encounter one another over the decades-spanning narrative.

Amazingly heroic characters need amazingly challenging obstacles. If not, life is all too easy for them. So Jean Valjean needs Inspector Javert, Ian Fleming's James Bond needs Blofeld, and Sir Arthur Conan Doyle's Sherlock Holmes needs Professor Moriarty. The more intriguing and cunning the villain, the more brilliant and extraordinary the hero has to be.

To really spice up a person-versus-person relationship, you have to go beyond simply hate, or simply love. Have them love *and* hate each other. Have them despise but need each other. Often you can discover an excellent character simply by imagining who your hero's perfect enemy, least-likely lover, or nightmare roommate would be.

NOPE

Create a scenario where a character has to achieve an incredibly simple task—flipping a switch, scratching her nose, sitting down for a cup of coffee.

As you write, every time she approaches that goal, throw a new obstacle in her path.

Be fierce. Be ruthless.

Watch how she digs herself out. Watch as her determination to achieve her goal rises to the level of the obstacle. Watch how she shines.

ELEVATOR

Imagine two characters diametrically opposed. Go small or big—God and Satan, playground bully and victim, ex-spouses.

Lock them in an elevator that's stuck between floors.

What are they going to talk about? What's going to happen?

Jump three days into the future.

Have them discover that the only food remaining is a single chocolate bar.

Let these characters talk, and act, and find out what they bring out in each other.

SUSPENSE!

Be your first reader. Do everything you can to make yourself laugh when you're writing, or sad, or unsettled, or creeped out. If you can't make yourself feel these things, it's hard to expect a random reader to feel them.

Manuel Gonzales

MAKE YOUR READER HUNGRY

Lee Child, the author of the popular Jack Reacher books, uses baking as an analogy to building suspense in fiction. In a piece for *The New York Times* called "A Simple Way to Create Suspense," Child suggests that asking how to bake a cake is the wrong question. The real question is how to make your guests hungry.

"And the answer is: You make them wait four hours for dinner."

His method is simple. Withhold information. Child compares this to a television show posing a question just before the commercial break knowing most of us will stick around to find the answer.

The craft book *Naming the World*, edited and largely contributed to by Bret Anthony Johnston, points to a higher level of suspense. Johnston dissects the haunting tale of Grover in the preschool classic *The Monster at the End of This Book* by Jon Stone. In the book, Grover is constantly pleading with us not to turn the pages of the book. The title has warned him: There's a monster at the end of this book! But like a wide-eyed Oedipus, we turn page after page. Our reading becomes the key action of the narrative. Johnston gleans some excellent craft wisdom from this book, including the nugget, "If your readers want something, do not give it to them."

Johnston, like Child, encourages us to whet the reader's appetite, allow their hunger to inspire their reading.

This won't work alone. If the only suspense in your novel is withheld information, you'll have plenty of readers simply skipping ahead. And let's face it, it's a weak meal that needs an hour delay to make you appreciate it. But if you can fill a room with the aroma of a cooking meal, if you can seduce your reader to stick around and have another glass of wine while their mouths water for the promised feast, then you've built a hunger ready to ravish your pages.

HITCHCOCK ON SUSPENSE AND SURPRISE

In the book *Hitchcock/Truffaut*, French filmmaker François Truffaut interviews the master of suspense, Alfred Hitchcock. The book is an excellent read for any fan of film or suspenseful narrative and gives delightful insight into Hitchcock's methodology.

More than once in the extended conversations, Hitchcock marks the difference between *surprise* and *suspense*. Hitchcock asks Truffaut to imagine a scene in which the two are sitting at a table chatting. From out of nowhere, a bomb explodes. The audience is just as surprised as the two men sitting at the table.

It works as a shock, but Hitchcock suggests there's a more satisfying way of building the moment.

Imagine the audience sees the bomb secretly placed under the table where the two men are sitting. As the men continue their conversation, ignorant of the danger they're in, the audience, Hitchcock argues, experiences something stronger than surprise. They experience suspense. They long to yell a warning to the screen—get away from that bomb! They wring their hands as seconds tick by, knowing that at any moment, the bomb will put an end to the two filmmakers' casual conversation.

"In the first case," Hitchcock explains, "we give the public fifteen seconds of *surprise* at the moment of the explosion. In the second we have provided them with fifteen minutes of *suspense*."

Hitchcock advises us to give our audience/readers all the information, even if our characters are left in the dark. He reveals as much information as he can, then lets his audience squirm, helpless to aid the characters on the screen.

But the master filmmaker doesn't dismiss the power of surprise. Anyone who has seen *Psycho* knows Hitchcock loves a well-orchestrated twist ending. In such cases Hitchcock states, "the unexpected ending is, in itself, the highlight of the story."

THE IMPOSSIBLE SITUATION

Put a character at a fork in the road. One route will lead to lifelong poverty for herself and her young child. The other road offers wealth and comfort, but she'll never see her child again.

Here the suspense is not built on withheld information. Nor is the suspense dependent on an approaching tragedy. It is simply the tension of an impossible situation.

This suspense has everything to do with being emotionally invested in a character. We ask ourselves as we greedily turn the page, not just *what will happen*, but *what will they do*, and perhaps *what would I do?*

A few things will help build this particular style of suspense.

First, the character must be in a position of choice and action. They must have options. The choices must be manifested in action and those actions must have consequences. Otherwise you have a character with no control over the path of the narrative.

The higher the stakes, the more intense the suspense. The more difficult the choice, the more forceful the pressure. Find a nearly impossible situation and watch your character reveal himself and your readers sweat the suspense.

Joel and Ethan Coen's first movie *Blood Simple* puts the decent-natured Ray into a nearly impossible situation.

Ray discovers the body of his former boss and believes his lover has committed the murder. Ray's a moral guy, but he doesn't want his lover to go to jail. The choice is a little difficult, but not insurmountable. Hoping to cover her tracks, Ray clumsily cleans up the crime scene, loads the body in a car, and drives out to the farm fields of Central Texas to bury the corpse.

But the man is not dead. As Ray watches in disbelief, the man crawls down the dark Texas highway coughing up blood.

Now Ray is trapped with two terrifying options. He can take the dying man, a despicable person, to the hospital, sending his lover and himself to jail. Or he can finish the job. More simply put, does he commit murder, or damn his lover?

It's an excruciating, dialogue-free sequence.

No information is withheld. No bomb is ticking. Instead we live in the skin of a character in an impossible situation. Two equally horrifying options lay before him. Both obvious and available.

If one option were the clear answer, the suspense would vanish.

If there were no consequences for either choice, the suspense would vanish.

If too much time or help is given the character, the suspense would vanish.

Instead he's in an impossible situation and must make a choice now, alone on the side of the highway.

Examples of impossible situations can be found in Toni Morrison's *Beloved*, William Styron's *Sophie's Choice*, and Roman Polanski's *Knife in the Water*. Craft the right kind of impossible situation and you'll rip a character in two…which is a great way to get a look inside.

THE UNTHINKABLE THIRD

Once you've built a scenario where a character must choose between two equally horrific options, you have the job of resolving the situation. Does the character choose *A* or *B*? Or does the character discover the unthinkable third—an option that up until that moment had not occurred to her or, ideally, the reader.

In the *Blood Simple* sequence described in "The Impossible Situation," Ray is unable to choose between murdering a man to save his lover from prison or saving the man. He can't save him and he can't kill him. He eventually embraces the unthinkable third. He buries the man alive.

The unthinkable third doesn't have to be that dark. In *The Incredibles*, Brad Bird sets up a struggle for Mr. Incredible. He can either be a superhero alone or a normal family man with his family. It's only in the film's third act that Elastigirl helps him realize that the dichotomy is false and the family can be superheroes together.

Often, the unthinkable third comes at the conclusion of the story. But it can also be the origin of a story. In *Tootsie* (Larry Gelbart and Murray Schisgal), Dustin Hoffman's character Michael Dorsey has a horrible reputation as an actor. He sees his two options as a) humble himself and become a more cooperative actor, or b) retire from acting altogether. He chooses the unthinkable third—dress as a woman and acquire an acting job under a false identity.

The unthinkable third can also work thematically. In Kate Chopin's short story "The Storm," a woman has an afternoon encounter with another man while her husband and son are away in town. The story seems to present the choice of marriage or infidelity. But by the story's end, the woman is enjoying dinner with her family and all the characters are content. The reader is left to ponder a reimagining of domestic tranquility.

Writing has the ability to weave in and out of the dualistic thinking to which we often default. When the character and/or the reader is placed in a situation where they believe only two paths are possible, the unthinkable third can be a refreshing surprise.

The trick is to allow the narrative to lead the character to discover the unthinkable third and prepare the reader for it without giving it away. When looking back on all that's come before, the story was always moving toward the unthinkable third. You're aiming for a conclusion that is surprising and immensely satisfying. As Aristotle pointed out in *Poetics*, an ending must be both unexpected *and* inevitable.

ALL THE OPTIONS

Create five simple scenarios in which a character is presented with what appears to be a two-path decision. We also have a few options here you can work with. Now go back through those, and spend time discovering what other options exist—what is the unthinkable third?

SOME IDEAS:

An egg falls out of the carton at the grocery store. Do you a) replace the egg and walk away quietly or b) admit it and offer to pay for the eggs?

Julie thinks she's alone inside an abandoned house. A voice, creepy and old, creaks, "Come upstairs." Does she a) go upstairs or b) get the hell out of there?

Sam discovers he's in love with his coworker. Does he a) admit his love and risk his work environment or b) keep it a secret?

REALITY, NEEDS, AND SNAPS

One thing I like about jazz, kid, is that I don't know
what's going to happen next. Do you?

Bix Beiderbecke

EXPECTATION VS. ACTUALITY

A man sits down expecting the chair to hold him. The chair holds him. No story there.

The man sits and the chair does not hold him.
Story.

As screenplay guru Robert McKee likes to say, "The story lies in the gap between expectation and reality."

A woman dives into the bay, expecting nothing but a midnight swim. In actuality, she meets a shark. *Jaws* (Peter Benchley, Carl Gottlieb).

A young boy expects nothing for his birthday. He instead gets an invitation to attend an academy for wizardry and witchcraft. J.K. Rowling's *Harry Potter* series.

A king expects love and devotion from his daughters. In actuality they are conniving and cruel, and it drives him mad. Shakespeare's *King Lear*.

When a character experiences exactly what they expected to experience, there's no surprise, there's no tension, and there's no dramatic action. This can be as simple as the above chair scenario, or as profound as a philosophical crisis of faith. The hero of Ralph Ellison's *Invisible Man* believes that if he follows the rules set forth by society, he will be rewarded. The novel is a series of realizations that his world is unjust, unfair, and most perplexing, inconsistent. Fitzgerald's Gatsby believes in true love. He is a romantic, and expects that his dedication to Daisy will be met with mutual love. When his romantic views meet up with the actuality of Daisy's pragmatism and greed,

Gatsby is destroyed.

The actuality doesn't always have to undermine the expectation. It can instead exceed it. Charlie in Roald Dahl's *Charlie and the Chocolate Factory* expects to find amazing delights inside Willy Wonka's chocolate factory. But the actuality of the chocolate factory far exceeds even his wildest dreams.

A writer can also play with the reader's expectations. Alfred Hitchcock's *Psycho* (Joseph Stefano) made brilliant use of the audience's expectations. Janet Leigh was clearly our hero—the movie star we would be following throughout the film. So when she is murdered in her shower thirty minutes into the film, the massive gap that forms between our expectations and actuality becomes the heart of the story.

Thwarted expectations can and should work on multiple levels simultaneously for both the reader and the characters.

Take this example:

A woman comes home early from a work trip expecting to find her husband happy to see her. If she got what she expected, we wouldn't have much of a story. Instead she finds him in bed with another person. In fact, it's the woman's brother.

The woman's expectations and beliefs have clashed with reality.

On the simplest level, she expected just her husband to be home.

She also expected her husband to be faithful, but in actuality he was not.

She expected her husband to be heterosexual, but in actuality he is not.

She expected that her marriage was stable, but in actuality it is not.

Now she must deal with a world that is radically different than what she had presumed. The gap between her expectations and actuality is forcing her into action. She must either try to correct the world to fit her expectations, come to peace with the actuality, or strike out on a new, previously unimagined path.

NEED VS. WANT

Life would be easier if what we wanted and what we needed lined up. But from the trivial—*I need nourishment; I want a donut*—to the significant—*I need the love of others; I want to be alone*—the tension between need and want heats our lives.

In *A Christmas Carol*, Charles Dickens' Scrooge *wants* money and solitude; he *needs* the joys of generosity and family. In Fyodor Dostoevsky's *Crime and Punishment*, Raskolnikov *wants* to be a "great man" above morality and free from consequences; he *needs* consequences and a higher truth to give his world meaning. In Donna Tartt's *The Goldfinch*, Theo *wants* to conceal Carel Fabritius' painting. He *needs* to heal the wounds left after his mother's death.

A character is usually aware of his or her want. They'll often state it quite plainly. Han Solo in George Lucas' *Star Wars: A New Hope* is very clear about his motives and desires. "Look, I ain't in this for your revolution, and I'm not in it for you, Princess. I expect to be well paid. I'm in it for the money." Raskolnikov repeats his want again and again. In *The Great Gatsby*, F. Scott Fitzgerald's hero is clear about his want. He wants Daisy and everything she represents.

Inversely our characters are often unaware of or unwilling to admit their need. In fact, they'll hint at their needs by declaring the opposite. When a character tells us, "I don't need anybody else. I'm better off alone," we understand what she *needs* is friends.

It's important that we can relate or at least forgive a character's *wants* even as we recognize his deeper *needs*. Gatsby's obsession is rooted in romantic love. Han Solo has to pay off Jabba the Hutt. It also helps that both these characters are charming. As in life, charm and humor help us forgive a great many faults,

It's possible to have a story where a character's need and want are one and the same. Think most superhero stories or James Bond novels. James Bond wants to save the world. James Bond needs to save the world. This can lead to a one-level story that is entertaining, but little else. The most successful—and we'd argue most entertaining—of Bond or superhero stories grapple with the tension between a character's wants and needs.

Often, but not always, the *want* represents the external desires of the character: lifestyle, career success, concrete goals. The *need* is the internal, deeper desire: love, balance, compassion. Perhaps because wants are external and so often vocalized, they appear to be the engine of the narrative. Maverick wants to win the Top Gun trophy, Kermit wants to score a Hollywood contract, and we are rooting for them to achieve their goals and acquire their wants.

The reader is invested in Theo's attempts to hide *The Goldfinch*; it seems to be what the story is "about." But a successful narrative pits the observable want against the more subtle and deeper needs of a character. Eventually, either the character reconciles their *needs* and *wants*, or comes to a point where they willingly abandon their wants in order to fulfill their needs, or the needs of their community.

The strength of your narrative is often dependent on this dichotomy. Create characters who have strong wants and compelling needs. Allow them to be torn in two directions. Deep wants, deep needs, deep conflict.

SNAP!

How do you snap? You push your fingers against each other in opposite directions. When a character's expectation pushes against the actuality, or a character's wants push against their needs, we have the opportunity for a narrative snap.

EXPECTATION / ACTUALITY SNAP

Any time a character's expectation fails to match reality, there is an opportunity for story. But when the opposition is strong enough, the clash resonates as a narrative snap. To work successfully, the character and the reader or viewer must have a belief so strong it is nearly unquestioned. This belief or expectation then confronts an equally strong actuality that must immediately be as unquestionable.

Take the ending of *Psycho*. Lila Crane descends into the basement expecting to find Mrs. Bates, Norman's mother. Instead she finds a not-so-preserved corpse, and is soon attacked by Norman, dressed as his mother. Her expectation, which we shared, slams against reality and creates a snap.

Any twist ending is a perfect example of an expectation/actuality snap. Consider the now-classic ending of M. Night Shyamalan's *The Sixth Sense*. Bruce Willis' Malcolm Crowe believes himself to be alive. It is a simple, fundamental, unquestioned belief. In the final moments of the film, he is forced to face the reality that he is indeed dead. In both *The Sixth Sense* and *Psycho*, the snap vibrates through the entire story, affecting not only the ending but compelling the viewer, like the character, to reexamine everything that has come before.

WANTS / NEEDS SNAP

When a character's *wants* and *needs* oppose each other, we get powerful tension. The deeper the *wants* and *needs*, the more intense the tension. Your job is to increase the tension. Don't make the *wants* less appetizing—that's too easy. Push a character in two opposite directions at once until they snap.

Let's go back to Han Solo. Han *wants* reward money. It's an external, concrete goal. And understandable—he's got to pay back Jabba the Hutt, a very dangerous guy. He believes his *want* is his most pressing *need*. But through the journey another possibility emerges. Maybe friendship and a higher cause are the deeper *needs*. Han stays loyal to his *want* throughout the film, barely hinting at the deeper call coming from within.

It's only in the final moments of the film that he and Chewie return to the battle against the Death Star, choosing to risk everything for their new friends and the righteous cause of the Rebellion. That moment when Han flies in to help Luke is a reversal, a surprise, a snap. The circumstances pushing his *wants* in one direction and his *needs* in another finally crack and we get the exciting reversal.

Not just a reversal of the character's individual direction, but also of the story's values. In Han's arc, greed and self-preservation are winning out over selflessness. Han turns his ship around, turns his own story around, and turns the arrow of value from selfishness to selflessness. SNAP!

Suzanne Collins' *The Hunger Games* has a series of snaps as Katniss goes against her own desire to survive in order to serve a deeper need of helping others. These snaps represent a threat to the value system of the established world and plant the seeds for the rebellion that will come to fruition by the end of the trilogy.

Sometimes it is the most personal of snaps, the most intimate of wants versus needs that drive a narrative. In *It's a Wonderful Life* (Frances Goodrich, Albert Hackett, and Frank Capra based on a story by Philip Van Doren Stern), George Bailey *wants* to live a free, independent life with no personal commitments; he *needs* Mary, his family, and the community of Bedford Falls. The writers push on George's frustration and desire to get the hell out of his little hometown. But they also confront him with Mary. She's charming, sharp, and beautiful. She's perfect for George. His need for her is dynamically opposed to his want to live free of relationship obligations.

In the scene portraying their first kiss, the situation becomes comically and dramatically intense for George. George is doing everything he can to deny his *need* for Mary. He's distant, rude, argumentative. Mary rightfully loses patience with him and it seems the two are doomed to forever be apart. But the writers aren't done. They force the two together, sharing one receiver for a phone call to a friend in New York. The two people who, at this moment, want to be far apart find themselves cheek-to-cheek. Now more than ever, George feels the dual drives of his need and want.

In a last ditch effort to preserve his wants, George grabs Mary by the shoulders and desperately proclaims, "I don't want to get married—ever—to anyone! You understand that? I want to do what I want to do. And you're... and you're... oh Mary, Mary." He's nearly yelling what he *wants*, but it's clear to us, and finally to him, what he *needs*. Both powers pushing until... SNAP. And the two embrace in their first kiss.

It's a Wonderful Life is filled with such snaps. A young George jumps into a frozen lake to save his brother, putting the need of his brother above his own desire for self-preservation. He gives up on attending college in order to run the struggling Savings and Loan. Only in the last third of *It's a Wonderful Life* do we and George realize that these snaps—both the public and personal—have had a huge impact on the world of Bedford Falls.

Sometimes the opposing forces that reveal a character are so great they crush the character. We've discussed the clash between the stern Inspector Javert and the valiant Jean Valjean in Victor Hugo's *Les Misérables*. The straightforward, external predicament of pursuer and pursued helps drive the story and motivate both characters. But a narrative snap in Javert's arc highlights his internal struggle.

The climax of Javert's arc is initiated by an unexpected act of kindness from Jean Valjean. Jean Valjean has Javert's life in his hands, but the former convict shows the inspector mercy and allows Javert to escape with his life.

Jean Valjean's act of compassion is so opposed to Javert's expectations that it throws him into an emotional and philosophical torrent. How could a criminal have shown him mercy? This new gap between expectations and actuality forces Javert's *want*—to arrest Jean Valjean—into sudden contention with his *need* to understand grace. How can he arrest the man who spared his life? But if he doesn't, how can he oppose the law he has sworn to uphold?

The tension is too great. Javert, torn between impossible choices, drowns himself in the waters of the Seine. It is a dark Unthinkable Third as Javert refuses to choose between the law and grace and instead destroys himself.

Narrative snaps make your prose pop and propel your story forward. Create opportunities where the deepest parts of a character and the way they see the world clash, pushing in opposite directions with such force that the sharp snap echoes through the pages.

SNAPS!

Your challenge is to come up with five two-sentence scenarios that feature a significant reversal or gap between expectation and reality.

EXAMPLE:

I'm pregnant. It's not yours.

Now write down five *want* vs. *need* scenarios.

EXAMPLE:

Shipwreck survivors in a lifeboat each *want* individual survival. They *need* the mutual support and cooperation.

When you go back and look through them, you might find that one is the perfect central snap for a story.

THE WHITE
HOT HEART

*One of the few things I know about writing is this:
spend it all, shoot it, play it, lose it, all, right away,
every time...give it, give it all, give it now.*

Annie Dillard

FINDING THE HEART

Stare into a fire, past the flames, within the tangle of logs and branches and you'll see a core—a center so hot the color bends blue. Stories have a heart just as hot. It may be an event, an urge, or a relationship. Think of the unquenchable lust and greed in the center of Nabokov's *Lolita*, the image of a girl falling into a muddy puddle in Faulkner's *The Sound and the Fury*, the brilliantly lit basement in Ralph Ellison's *Invisible Man*.

Often the hot heart of your story is not what you expected. Sometimes it is only a revision read or the insight of a close reader that tells you what sets your story on fire. You thought your book was about class distinction or environmental crimes, but you find—or your closest readers reveal to you—that the hot center is a relationship between two characters.

Once you find it—the hot heart of your piece—tend it.

FEED THE FIRE

Sometimes the best way to increase the heat is to feed the fire by adding details, secrets, characters, even props to exacerbate the dramatic situation.

Many critics argue that the hot heart of *Hamlet* is the troubled prince's odd and intimate relationship with his mother. In a play that burns brilliantly, the scenes between Hamlet and Gertrude are nearly too hot to touch.

In Act 3 Scene 4, Hamlet and his mother have a heated argument in her bedroom chambers. Accusations of murder and infidelity sizzle in the presence of Gertrude's bed. This alone makes for an intense scene. But Shakespeare, not one to leave well-enough alone, adds fuel to the fire. He places Polonius hiding behind a drape spying on the raving prince. Now Hamlet's rage and the heat of the scene have some new logs to burn. Hamlet hears Polonius behind the drape. Believing this may be his murderous uncle, Hamlet stabs Polonius through the curtain.

This doesn't end the scene. Instead it makes the fire explode. Hamlet's lines here are some of the most powerful of the play. It takes Hamlet's dead dad's ghost appearing to cool things down.

The fuel you add to the fire can be a memory, a person, or an element of the environment. It can be traumatic, as in *Hamlet*, or a simple annoyance. A man sits at a bar slowly drinking himself into a depressed stupor. Have a persistent mosquito buzz about his ear. Let the humidity of the day bake him until he sweats whiskey. Have a phone ring continuously in some back room.

Often the heart of your story is deep, hidden under the action. The kindling you lay atop the hidden hot coals of your story can allow the visible flames to flash into life.

The hot core of Ernest Hemingway's "Hills Like White Elephants" is an unplanned pregnancy. The pregnancy is never explicitly mentioned. Instead the couple have a drink, wait for a train, and talk around the possibility of an abortion. How the couple discuss the drinks they are served and the appearance of the distant landscape provide the dry kindling, allowing the hidden heat of the story to burst into small but intense visible flames.

A writer's job includes keeping a near constant eye out in their day-to-day life for intriguing details, snippets of conversation, and other fun bits and pieces to add to the fire. Some of us fill pocket-sized notebooks, some suffice with mental notes and others rely completely on imagination. However we do it, we are collecting kindling for the blaze.

Of course, as with kindling to the flame, too many details can suffocate the story. Some writers pour on as much description and characters as the page will allow and find their writing is cold and lifeless. It's a process of give and take and trial and error. But eventually you'll find just the right amount of good burning fuel to feed your fire.

FIGHT THE FIRE

Sometimes you don't need to feed the fire, you need to fight it. Get in close and try to blow it out, stick the bellows into the fireplace and pump in some cold air. The very action that will extinguish a weaker flame provides oxygen for a flame strong enough to use it.

Get in the way of your characters. Stop them from doing what they want to do. As we talked about in "Torture your Character," the characters will rise to the challenge of their obstacles.

There are plenty of ways to fight the fire. Take away time, demanding that your characters achieve their goals before the ticking clock runs out. Watch as your characters move faster and more intensely than you and they believed possible.

Or injure a character. Take away their strongest asset.

Reveal a traitor in their midst who ruins their perfectly thought-out plan.

In *The Martian*, author Andy Weir did everything he could to kill off his stranded astronaut. Whenever things got a little too easy for Mark Watney all alone on Mars, Weir made sure to fan the flames. He impales Watney, blows him up, and threatens him with starvation. We read on, captivated by the flickering flame, wondering if this last gust of wind will blow it out. But the flame survives. In fact, it burns all the brighter.

Take a scene where two characters are eager to make love. They walk into the bedroom, already a tangle of arms. They move toward the bed. It's got heat, but needs a little more fire. Don't add mood lighting or a Sade soundtrack.

Instead, make the phone ring. It's an obstacle that would kill the mood of a mild tryst. One of the lovers throws the phone against the wall. "No interruptions tonight." Things heat up.

They fall onto the bed and it breaks. They smile, but don't slow down.
Someone yells, pounding on the front door.
They ignore it too, lost in the moment.
Smoke starts to drift through the AC vents.
They hold their breath and continue.
Flames climb the walls as sirens wail outside.
The couple never even peek above the sheets. They're still going at it as firefighters burst in and carry them from the blaze.

That's a hot scene. Every attempt to slow or stop their lovemaking only gives them a reason to pursue it with more vigor. We fight the fire and watch it grow.

TOO HOT TO TOUCH

Sometimes the hot heart of your story is an absence.

The Holy of Holies was the center of the ancient Temple in Jerusalem. It was believed to hold the presence of the Divine and was to be entered only with reverence and at great risk. Once a year, the priest entered alone, passing through the many outer sections of the Temple to the glowing core of the Jewish world. His disciples would tie a rope to his ankle so if he were struck dead by the holiness of God, his corpse could be recovered. It is a holy that must be approached but never entered. A heart so white hot it cannot be touched.

Kurt Vonnegut wrote *Slaughterhouse Five* to describe the terrors of the firebombing of Dresden, Germany. His hero, Billy Pilgrim, floats in time, traveling to his childhood, to his own death as an older man, to a distant planet, to his early days as a soldier and as a prisoner of war. He describes the days before the firebombing and the days immediately after. But he hardly touches the bombing itself. His hero is huddled inside a shelter, blind to the destruction happening above him.

Vonnegut understands that to try to describe the actual firebombing would never do it justice. Allowing that center to be empty is the finest way to represent the horror and power of the tragedy.

By jumping in time, Vonnegut touches every spot but one—the burning center too hot to touch. He gives us the shape of the heart by depicting its borders. And he demonstrates the heat of the heart by leading us as close as we can go and inviting us to hold out our open-palmed hands and feel the fire.

COUNTDOWN

This exercise is based on an improv game. On stage, we'd create a two-minute scene based on an audience suggestion. After the scene ended, we'd challenge ourselves to recreate the entire scene in half the time—one minute. Once we finished that scene, we'd get the same challenge again—can you do this scene in thirty seconds? Can you do it in fifteen seconds? Can you do it in seven seconds? Now in three seconds? And finally, can you recreate that scene in just one second? By the time we reached that point, each actor would jump to their character's single quintessential line and action and we'd culminate in a hilarious stage picture that also fully captured the energy and highlights of the original two-minute scene.

You can do the same with writing that you're worried is too wordy, not on target. Take the original chunk of text and try to rewrite it in half the space. If it was a twenty-page chapter, force yourself to rewrite it in only ten pages. Then rewrite it again in five pages. Then two-and-a-half pages.

At this point, see if you can capture the chapter in one page. In one paragraph. In one sentence. Get down and discover the white hot heart of the story.

HAPPY ENDINGS AND COMPLEX CLIMAXES

Sometimes writing is running downhill, your fingers jerking behind you on the keyboard the way your legs do when they can't quite keep up with gravity.

Rainbow Rowell

ENDINGS

ENDINGS AND BEGINNINGS

A brilliant flight can be ruined by an inept landing. It doesn't matter how tasty the inflight meals or polite the flight attendants were, if the plane crashes on touchdown, the flight is a failure. So work hard to nail your endings.

Know it or not, you begin writing your ending early into your first draft. The early questions, the Inciting Incident knocking the world/character off balance—these set you moving toward that surprising and inevitable ending. The ending hides in those early pages. It's a secret your writing is moving toward. Some writers will struggle for months on the ending of their story, but their answer lies in those first pages. As director/writer Billy Wilder put it, "If you have a problem with the third act, the real problem is in the first act."

This doesn't mean you must know your ending before you begin. Not at all. Many of us are writing to discover our ending. But understand that your ending and your beginning are sisters. They may fight, clash, and try to annihilate one another, but they share the same DNA.

As you write and revise, understand that relationship between your opening beats and the climactic conclusions. Hold the two close together and see if the questions (narratively, emotionally, and thematically) addressed in the beginning are considered in the conclusions. Do you recognize an arcing connection that bends above plot and connects the beginning and ending? This is your way of getting an idea of what your project is about.

This doesn't mean that the ending is what a character (or the reader) would expect from the early action of the story. Quite the opposite, in fact. The beginning and ending are sisters, but not twins. If you were to whisper the ending to the hero at the story's beginning, the hero would be surprised. Even when a character accomplishes the very dream the voices in the opening pages, it is through a means previously unimagined. She arrived where she was aiming for, but the path and transformation on the journey were unexpected.

ENDINGS AND MIDDLES

In the middle of your story hides magic. It is hidden in the struggle, in the love, in the loss in the middle of the journey. It is what Joseph Campbell calls *the elixir*. At the end of the journey, the hero puts the magic to use to defeat the monster and heal the unbalanced world.

The magic can take several forms. It's an acquired skill, the emotional growth, the hidden wisdom, or an actual physical tool. Sometimes the magic is unrecognized by the hero at the time. It's a failure or a scar, and its true worth only reveals itself in the story's ending.

Whatever the magic of the middle is, it is essential. Without it, the hero would fail in the final challenge.

Often the middle of a novel, memoir, or screenplay seems to digress into action off the path of the overarching plot. A new obstacle appears, a side adventure presents itself, or an obsession distracts the hero from her quest. But even the digressive mini-arcs must contribute to the hero's journey—externally and internally. It is in these arcs that our hero discovers the magic, the elixir.

Little Miss Sunshine (Michael Arndt) has a wonderfully magical ending. The family has achieved their goal of delivering innocent Olive to the titular children's beauty contest only to find it is a nasty, shallow, exploitative competition. In the talent portion of the contest, Olive performs a hilariously inappropriate dance routine, and her father Richard (Greg Kinnear) is sent to remove her from the stage. But he doesn't. Instead, he joins her on stage, and the rest of the family follows.

It's magic. And a new family balance is achieved.

If they had been able to fly out to the contest and avoid the long, misadventurous drive in their decrepit VW bus, Richard never would have had the humility and heroic sensibility to join his daughter in dancing. He found that humility and heroism—that magic—in the struggles of the journey. The family would have failed had it not been for the journey, just as Police Chief Brody would not have been able to kill the shark in *Jaws* or Frodo would have failed to bring the Ring to the edge of the fires of Mount Doom.

The setbacks, failures, and digressions of the middle of the journey prepare your hero for the challenge in the concluding beats of the story. If your characters were able to meet that final challenge without the lessons learned and obstacles overcome in the middle sections of your story, then your structure is flawed. Don't force them to undertake a journey to gain magic they do not need. The hero requires the challenges of the plot to discover the magic and grow into a person able to meet the ultimate challenge of the finale.

ENDINGS AND ENDINGS

There comes a moment near the conclusion of a narrative after which all things will have changed. The hero faces her greatest challenge, her most difficult obstacle or foe. The magic is used and balance found. The world is healed, often better, or at least wiser, than it was in the beginning.

The common term for this moment is climax, but we break the moment down into two beats: Crisis and Climax.

The Crisis is often a quiet moment in a narrative. It is an internal, intimate moment when a radical change happens within a character, but before the change has rippled out to the world at large. Though the approaching Climax might involve the fate of the universe, the crisis is of deep personal importance.

This is a moment not of major action, but of major decision. Luke Skywalker steers his X-Wing through the canyons and crevasses of the Death Star's surface. But it's not the explosions rattling around him or the TIE Fighters on his tail that spur the Crisis moment. The Crisis is spurred by a quiet voice from within. Luke hears the voice of his mentor urging him to turn off his computer and trust the Force. Here the philosophical and emotional conflict finds its conclusion. Luke will trust the Force over accepted technology. Though the Death Star still looms, the internal monster has been defeated. Once Luke turns his computer off, the Crisis has been answered and he is ready to face the Climax.

We all recognize the Climax. Buildings explode. Couples kiss. Heroes sacrifice themselves. Battles end. Aliens are blown to tiny little green bits. This is the moment that could not have been successfully faced by the character until they had endured the adventure of the narrative. The big decision of the crisis vibrates out into the world as big action.

In these final moments, the world experiences a radical reversal—sometimes positive, sometime negative. Kings become blind, homeless wanderers as in Sophocles' *Oedipus Rex*. An impoverished orphan finds a wealthy, loving family as in Charles Dickens' *Oliver Twist*.

The key to changing the world is knowing the levels of the world. What's at stake? What is impacted by the action of the Climax?

Think of it as concentric circles. The innermost circle is the personal—how is the individual changed? The hero? The next circle is the interpersonal. The friends, lovers, and intimate enemies of the hero—how are these relationships impacted? Next is societal. How has the Climax changed the workings of society? The final circle can be overall value. The positive or negative value of the world.

As we enter the final minutes of *It's a Wonderful Life*, George Bailey is a suicidal, jail-bound man. But he discovers his desire to live in the Crisis beat. The rest of the film illustrates the ripple effect of this personal change. He runs to his children and wife, his interpersonal world, and embraces them, laughing and kissing them. Next all the people of his community—his society—rush in, willingly filling his table with money to repay the bank's missing refunds. Finally, his brother raises a toast and declares George "the richest man in town." The crowd cheers and we see that the value system has reversed. It is this man with little money and many friends who is rich, while the wealthiest citizen of Bedford Falls is forgotten. In just a few minutes, George's internal victory is manifested in his family, community, and world values.

Let's return to the Climax of *Little Miss Sunshine*. As Richard Hoover breaks into a dance with his daughter, he demonstrates an internal change. That ripples to the rest of the family as they join him in dancing with Olive. We understand as they all dance together that they are healed. It's not said, but we understand there won't be a divorce. Nor will the son run away. The larger societal pressure of the beauty contest is thrown into chaos as the family dances. Suddenly the system of the beauty contest and the values it promoted are overturned. Inward authenticity and family love trump outward success. In a sense, the world will never be the same.

MARKING THE BEATS

Pick three of your favorite narratives—novels, films, stories, memoirs. Quickly jot down the basic beats—not a summary, just a sentence or two each to capture the critical moments of the story. Make sure to find the Inciting Incident, the Crisis, the Climax, and the resolution.

Being able to recognize these in other stories will help you as you craft these moments into your own.

REVISION AND WRITER'S BLOCK

You play. You win. You play. You lose. You play.

Jeanette Winterson

PUT IT AWAY

Now you have a finished draft. It's unwieldy, too long or too short, character arcs fade into nowhere, tone is a tangled mishap. It's a fermenting pile of word vomit.

Or you've finished the draft and you're convinced it's perfect! You've written every word perfectly the first time round. Don't even bother with spellcheck. It's done, baby!

Either way, step back. Put it in a drawer, close the file. Go do something else entirely. Start another book or learn a new language or take a hike. Give it time to marinate.

Some authors wait a month. Others a week. For shorter pieces (with quickly approaching deadlines) it may be a few hours. Whatever the case, some time allows you to see the words with new eyes. New eyes are exactly what you need for revision. Revision means to look again—to see again. Those weeks, days, or hours give you the time to see it all afresh.

Chances are the pages are not nearly as bad or good as you had initially thought. And those new eyes can see exactly the steps you need to take to carry the project across the finish line. At this point, you have permission to invite your internal editor to join the process. Read, cut, slice, fix, tweak, edit. Read it again. You'll recognize many of these suggestions and techniques from the beginning of the writing process. The same methods that inspire a new project can also help untangle a stuck project or give us those new eyes to see a project we've been living with for months or maybe years.

Your new goal is an actual first draft, a draft you'd feel comfortable sharing with your innermost circle, your first reader, your writing group.

MESSED UP DRAFT

OWEN

Often when I've been working on an essay, a story, or a novel for so long, I reach a point where I'm not sure what to do next. It's become more polished, more revised, but somehow something is missing and I feel stuck.

This is when it's time for The Messed Up Draft.

First I take my working draft and click "Save as…" I append "messedup-draft" to the regular file name. Now my manuscript is still saved in its original state—it's safe, I'm not touching it. But the file in front of me is all mine. I'm free to do whatever the hell comes to mind. I can kill off the main character in chapter two. I can remove fifty pages from the middle. I can cut out all of my favorite parts, my best writing. I can cut the parts I'd be crazy to cut. I can scatter the chapters any which way, I can change the point of view, I can do nearly anything because I have the freedom to mess with this draft.

I can approach revision with the same abandon that I approached the first draft. The same freedom to put the inner critic aside and let anything go. When we've been working on a piece, especially something like a full book, which takes so long to write, the chapters that we're working on, revising, rereading again and again and again seem to become inevitable—we can't imagine the book without them. The messed up draft frees us from the illusion that what we've been writing can't change completely. It allows us the freedom to experiment and fail, and get messy. When we're not afraid to break this delicate thing we've been building, big discoveries appear. The book can surprise us, even in the act of revision. And you don't have to worry, even if you do break your precious draft, you've got your initial one waiting safely in another file....

THE POWER OF PLAY

Sometimes the best way to move forward when you're stuck is to move to the side. These exercises will help you through the muck of writer's block, when the words all feel wrong and the answers remain elusive.

All of these ideas are inspired by our work in improvisation. Many of our favorite improv games ask the performers to take a story and revisit it from wildly different perspectives. In these exercises, you'll set aside the draft you've already written, and explore your characters, your narrative, your plot points, your relationships, and your story from unexpected new angles. While the writing that comes out of these exercises may not end up in your book, the ideas and sparks that come from these explorations can drive the energy of your revision process.

Dive in. Surprise yourself. Surprise your characters. Come play.

PLAY WITH CONVENTIONS OF A GENRE OR MEDIUM

Try retelling a section of your story as if it were in a different genre. Tell it as a romance, a sci-fi, a mystery. Write it up as a legal brief. Craft it into a series of tweets. Transform it into a front-page newspaper article.

This approach can help you untangle a stuck scene. You've written that dialogue five times and it still feels stale. What if you write it in the style of a 1950s noir? A steamy bodice-ripper? Something you'd read in *Cosmopolitan* or *National Geographic*?

Playing with the conventions of a genre can give you a lot of freedom— readers know what to expect from a romance novel, and writers can target their words and sentences to meet these audiences. Sometimes the best way to find out your own book's expectations is to play around and target it to other audiences.

PLAY WITH VOICE

Sometimes writers struggle to identify their own narrative voice. It's hard to separate yourself from the sentences, and one way in is to play with voice.

Try writing your story using different narrators. Tell your story while channeling your favorite authors. How would Kurt Vonnegut write this scene? J.K. Rowling? Dr. Seuss?

Pick a narrative voice you know well, even if they're not an author. How would your story read if it were written by the president, or your favorite teacher, or your worst date, or your hilariously wacky great aunt?

Write as if you'd downed a ton of coffee, or a pile of sugar, or…choose your favorite vice.

Change the voice of each paragraph, and explore the sentences you create, the words you choose, that vary from your defaults.

PLAY WITH POINT OF VIEW

Another way in to a story that feels stuck is to try writing from the perspective of a different character. A writer knows her protagonist inside and out, can see that character's worldview in any scenario. But sometimes that character's view doesn't open up all of the nuances of the story.

Think of the *Harry Potter* series if we saw everything through Draco Malfoy's eyes.

How does *The Little Mermaid* change if you tell it from Ursula's perspective?

What would *Hamlet* be if Horatio were the narrator?

What if a bowl of porridge told the story of Goldilocks?

Let yourself discover your story anew. Be open to what you learn.

PLAY WITH AUDIENCE

Tinker with your story by shifting its audience—what would change about the words you'd choose if your audience were a class of kindergarteners?

What if your grandmother asked you to tell her the main love story?

What if you told your story over dinner to a blind date?

What areas would you emphasize; what words would you choose?

Write a version as if you've been asked to write it for your favorite magazine—How would your approach to your story change if you wrote it for *The New York Times Magazine*, *Reader's Digest*, *Cat Fancy*?

Then take some time to explore your actual intended audience—the people who will pick up your book and read it. Unpack the expectations they have about the style, the tone, your word choice or subject matter. Kurt Vonnegut spoke of every writer having one particular reader. For him, it was his sister. When he wrote, he imagined how she would understand the words—was he making his points clearly enough? Imagining a particular reader compelled him to be a more precise writer.

Don't write to a vacuum—write to your readers.

PLAY WITH SETTING / TIME PERIOD

Explore what happens if you take your manuscript and rewrite it in a different time period, a different setting.

How would it change if it were based in Victorian England? On a cruise ship? On a seemingly-abandoned space station?

Some of our most enduring stories benefit from such re-visions—Romeo and Juliet have died together in Elizabethan England, contemporary Manhattan, Cold War-era Russia, and in a suburban backyard as garden gnomes (though…spoiler alert, Gnomeo and Juliet don't die).

While most likely this exploration won't result in you crafting a space western instead of your literary fiction, you'll likely find some new surprises that can work their way into your narrative.

PLAY WITH EMOTION

Sometimes powerful new writing emerges when you add an emotion onto the scene. Rewrite a scene of your book but infuse it with sadness, exhilaration, terror, joy, resignation.

Give one of your characters a deep, dark secret. You never have to explain it, just infuse it into the way you see that character, and see what happens.

The next time you walk through the grocery store, try dropping a layer of emotion on top of your fellow shoppers. The professor choosing carrots is overcome with despair. The parent selecting a box of noodles is bursting with glee. The cashier is terrified. Suddenly they have stories, an active, rich life that exists outside of this moment. Suddenly they're not the background of your mundane errands—they're alive.

READ IT AGAIN FOR THE FIRST TIME

You've been working with these words for so long, they're as familiar to you as your favorite worn-in jeans. How to get distance in order to edit?

NEW TOOLS, OLD TOOLS

One fun way to jumpstart your revision process is to use a medium different than your go-to writing medium. If you usually open your laptop and start on a blank screen, try pulling out a pad of paper and writing longhand. If you usually write in pencil, eraser at the ready, see what happens with a pen.

If you need less formality and more playfulness, try writing with crayons or markers. So many adults believe they cannot draw, believe that they draw like a child. Why? Because most of us stopped getting art lessons in elementary school, middle school. We draw like kids because we stopped learning. But those drawings? They still rock. Let yourself draw a robot, a unicorn, a baby monkey. Enjoy that drawing, and connect to the person who wasn't told they couldn't draw. Validate your inner doodler. Embrace color, texture, motion. Feel your words on the page.

Perhaps our favorite writing medium for channeling your writerly inspiration: a vintage typewriter. The older the better. With a typewriter, you must release your impulse to edit, correct, overthink as you write. You have some options to go back and xxx out words, but mostly, what you write is what remains on the page. It's tactile, visceral—you can feel the indentation of the letters pressed into the page. You have to use force to depress the key and send the hammer flying into the ribbon. And it looks striking, official, legit. Type your name on a crisp piece of parchment paper, and you will feel like a writer. Own that feeling. Claim your words.

VISUAL UPDATE

Sometimes the key to getting a bit of space from your work is as simple as changing the way they look on the page. If you have a standard typeface or font you usually write in, select-all and try out a different one. Replace your Times New Roman with Garamond, Book Antiqua, Georgia. Choose something vastly different like sans-serif Arial and see how it feels to read. The font you use often becomes your digital handwriting, and your words will feel fresh with a new style of lettering. Even Comic Sans…if you must.

Or try changing the color of the words—read your book in purple, or rich brown. Flip it and have white words on a blue background. You won't necessarily publish it this way; you're just trying to jostle yourself, clear the part of your brain that already expects the next words and next ideas it knows you wanted to write.

Another method is to prose-poem your words—make each sentence into its own line. You won't likely want to undertake this challenge for a whole book, but for a section that feels stunted or off, playing with the layout on the page can help you read it afresh.

READ ALOUD

One of our favorite methods for diving into revision is reading your draft out loud. Imagine that your work has been released as an audiobook, and you're the narrator. Yes, it may feel awkward at first. Power through—it's worth it. Hearing your words brings your book to life, and it also allows you fresh entry into the project.

As you read, hold a highlighter in your hand, or have the highlighter tool ready on the screen. Don't edit as you go, just note the places you know you'll need to return to.

Your sentences, and your dialogue especially, should read naturally as you read them aloud. If you find yourself stumbling, if you find that you have to read a sentence twice to get the syntax, or if the dialogue sounds stilted, mark those sentences—those are the ones you're going to want to revise.

REVERSE OUTLINE

A reverse outline can help you spot patterns and problems in your narrative. Many writers love the structure and order of an outline—lay out the framework for your piece, and then follow it as a guide as you write. A reverse outline is less scaffolding and more discovery. You create it from the work you've already written.

The simplest way to create a reverse outline is to open a new document, read through your book, and jot down a quick plot summary at the end of each chapter. You'll end up with your whole project distilled to its key points, much easier to flip through than the entire manuscript.

You can go as close as you'd like—some reverse outlines capture the key points of each chapter, some drill deeper and go paragraph by paragraph, or section by section. Jotting down what happens in each section can help you spot holes, repetition, and themes, and can help you pinpoint sections lacking action or power or stakes.

If you have a chapter that's just not working, you might make a reverse outline of just that chapter. After each paragraph, jot down what happened in a few words. By the end of the chapter, you'll have a snapshot of the action.

With quick notes rather than full paragraphs, you can play with the organization of the text. Create your reverse outline on a series of notecards—ready to be shuffled and shifted. Or print out and cut up your outline notes, then see what happens if you rearrange them. Organize the notes by character and read through each individual's arc. Move the big reveal further down in the book, or pull it back much earlier. Put the entire book into chronological order, or mix it up to include flashbacks after the midpoint. You have the power to recreate your book without having to rewrite…yet.

HIGHLIGHTERS

Some writers see their work best in technicolor. Go through your piece—or your summary—and make every encounter between your protagonist and antagonist highlighted in purple. Or highlight a character you worry might be underdeveloped.

Then zoom out so you can barely read the type—try setting the zoom to 10%. Your screen will show an array of pages, and what you'll see mostly are the bands of color. Take some time to scroll through the project—where are the color blocks thick? Where are there gaps? You'll get a visual map of your book, color-coded.

Some writers will be able to track many colors at once—others may need to process just one color at a time.

MINDMAPS

Alternately, try creating some mindmaps of your book. Mindmaps help you break free of linear text to see your work anew.

Put your main character in the middle, create a node for the other characters in the book, and map the highlights of their relationships. Which relationships feel more fully realized? Do some need additional attention?

Put the title of your book in the middle, create a node for each chapter, and map out the plot—are there some chapters that are very plot intensive, while others seem spare?

Create a node for your subplots and map them out. Do they all have a full, satisfying arc?

This is another area where there's no right answer—you're not looking to have a mindmap where all the nodes have an equal number of points. You're really looking to see if the book you've written is the book you think you've written—if you believe that the critical relationship is between your protagonist and her true love, but you discover that most of the key moments of intensity and emotion happen between the protagonist and her mother, that's a place to explore further as you revise.

TABLES AND CHARTS

You can expand this process by making a table or chart—if you swoon at spreadsheets, this section is for you. If the thought of rows and columns makes you itchy, move along to the next chapter, no worries.

Create a table in your word processor or in your favorite spreadsheet program.

Each row represents a chapter (or paragraph, or section, depending on your piece), and each column represents something you want to track—individual characters, relationships, key plot points, places where there are reveals and reversals, points of conflict or clashes of values.

Sometimes you might track an element simply with an "x" in the cell—if you want to know each chapter in which a minor character appears. Other elements may require more details—noting what secrets get revealed, or the state of a relationship.

If you're taking on a large-scale project—a fantasy novel with significant world-building—a chart can help you keep track of everything from the terrain of the different lands to the critters that live there. When you're two hundred pages into your revision and you don't recall the color of the squid-centaur's tentacles, you'll be able to flip to your chart rather than digging through thousands of words of text.

FRESH EYES

The words are swirling and you just can't look at it one more time—it's time to bring in other readers. You want to find some trusted readers who'll be able to give you honest, clear feedback.

Warning—not all willing readers are good readers. Some readers are all too enthusiastic, thrilled that you were able to put so many words on paper that they have no eyes to see the flaws (i.e., your mother). Other readers see nothing but flaws. It can be particularly difficult for a fellow writer who's in the process of developing his own voice to read a colleague's manuscript and not critique it for failing to be the book he would have written. Choose your readers well. Handpick one to three early readers. Eventually you'll be a best seller and everyone can read this book. Have patience.

When you give your reader your draft, lay out some specific areas for them to respond to. We like asking readers to annotate their draft with comments as they go, either commenting in the margins on a hard copy or using the "comment" feature in most word processing programs or in Adobe Reader.

Ask them to note places where they stumble, places where they're totally drawn in and can't put it down, and places where they find themselves skimming or zoning out. Also ask them to highlight any sentence they had to read more than once to grasp the meaning—you'll definitely want to revise those.

We also like to have readers give us a running commentary on the narrative—who do they see as the culprit? Why? What do they think of the characters? If you're trying to make one character seem likeable, only to pull the rug out and reveal him as the evil overlord, get your reader to track their thoughts on that character as they read. If you're worried you're giving too many clues—or too few—your reader's comments can provide key feedback.

You also might want to point out areas where you don't need feedback just yet—if you're still untangling some plot points, you don't need sentence-level editing. Often, seeing a draft marked up with punctuation and word change suggestions will distract you from the larger revision work that needs your attention. Get the characters solid and true, nail down their journeys and transformations, and then go back to make sure you have the correct use of it's.

Once you have their feedback, you can sit down and untangle the suggestions. Some may make obvious sense. Some will seem clearly wrong. And many might open more questions than answers. This is all good. Look for the patterns—if two of your readers hated one key scene, and the other thought it was the best moment of the book, you know that at the very least you need to dive back in to that scene and explore it further.

Getting a reader's eye view into your manuscript can be just the recharge you need to dive into revisions.

TINKERING, TWEAKING, AND POLISHING

Interviewer: How much rewriting do you do?
Hemingway: It depends. I rewrote the ending of Farewell to Arms, the last page of it, 39 times before I was satisfied.
Interviewer: Was there some technical problem there? What was it that had stumped you?
Hemingway: Getting the words right.

Ernest Hemingway, *The Paris Review*

DIVING BACK IN

Revising your work takes place at multiple levels. Most of our discussion so far has been about revising at the narrative or story level—exploring the characters, their relationships, the narrative arc of the book. In this chapter we're exploring some techniques for fine-tuning—dive in here once the story's in place and it's time to tinker with paragraphs, sentences, and words.

There are so many fantastic books out there already about sentence-level revision strategies. We'll share a few ideas to get you started here, but if you leave inspired to study further, here are some of our favorites. For an engaging, conversational read, try *Writing with Style* by John Trimble. For a step-by-step approach, check out Richard Lanham's *Revising Prose* and learn his Paramedic Method of reducing the "lard factor" of your prose.

Ultimately, revising sentences is a balancing act. The rules are slippery, and should be understood and broken. You can write perfect but stagnant sentences, and you can write sloppy but vibrant sentences.

We're all shuffling the same deck of words. Let's find some ways to choose the most effective ones to tell your story.

ONE IDEA, ONE PARAGRAPH

When in doubt, keep your paragraphs short. Readers use paragraphs for pacing, and to note a shift in ideas. Try to keep yourself to one idea per paragraph. Three four-sentence paragraphs are usually more readable than one long twelve-sentence block of text.

In the workshops we teach, we present two pages with identical text. The only difference is that one page is one continuous paragraph and the other is broken up into several small paragraphs. We ask the students to pick which they'd rather read—which page looks more inviting and welcomes them in. The page with the multiple paragraphs is always the favorite. Remember, the words are identical, but the paragraph breaks offer a more inviting rhythm. The breaks are the breaths between thoughts, the coffee breaks that allow our brain to enjoy the text.

If you find yourself looking at page-long paragraphs on your screen, go through and mark any shifts—in topic, tone, idea, focus. Start a new paragraph at each of those spots. Your reader will thank you.

Action sequences especially want short, sharp paragraphs to punctuate the energy of the scene. Each new paragraph pushes the reader forward, and the momentum of the reading experience matches the momentum of the story.

When you're close on a section but it's just not feeling right, sometimes the culprit is paragraph organization—you might have all the words there, but they're not in the right order.

This is when it's time to get down to basics. Print the section out, cut it into paragraphs, sit down on the floor and shuffle those paragraphs around.

Flip your first and last paragraphs, and see what happens.

As your story gels, it's finally time to turn your attention to the words.

CLEAR THE CLUTTER

To reach your readers with the most effective writing, aim for clarity—concise, clear sentences with strong, vibrant words. You're searching for the sweet spot here—the point where the rules of grammar and convention meet with your own writing voice.

As you revise your prose, pay attention to your patterns—the phrases you return to, the sentence styles you repeatedly craft. Some of that is your voice. And some of that is your default. Keep the sentences that make your voice shine. Revise the ones that feel repetitive and lifeless.

Sometimes a writer mistakes complicated structure for complex thought. This is something that's permeated our culture, that certain sentences "sound" smart—you can go far on some standardized tests if you know how to craft a convoluted sentence. But we're crafting stories, and clarity is key. As jazz genius Charles Mingus once said, "Making the simple complicated is commonplace; making the complicated simple, awesomely simple, that's creativity."

Keep your thoughts complicated, make your sentences simple.

THE JOY OF DELETE

With so many words to choose from, it's often tempting to use them all. But like a wall with too many pieces of art crammed onto it, a cluttered sentence is less than the sum of its parts. Choose the details we need, not every detail that exists.

There is a misconception that more details paint a more vivid picture. Writers are not just reporters of the facts, we are curators—our voice is defined as much by what we choose not to say as by what we say. Leave the inexhaustible list of details for a police report. Trim down to the most vivid essentials for prose. This is true on the story level and on the sentence level.

Compare this:

> Lucy turned on her manual transmission 2010 brown and cream Fiat convertible, let her left foot press on the clutch for two seconds while her right hand used the shifter to move the transmission into first gear as her left hand turned the steering wheel and she accelerated up to forty-five miles per hour over the course of the first second of driving.

With this:

> Lucy peeled out in her Fiat convertible.

In the first sentence, the key image—peeling out in the car—is lost in the unnecessary details, so that the strength of the image is diluted. And since the action itself is fast, sleek, moving, the sentences should match.

Compare this:

Visualize if you will a mental picture of one individual engaged in the intellectual activity of trying to ascertain what the rules and regulations are for how to play the ancient game that we now refer to as Tic-Tac-Toe.

With this:

Picture someone learning the rules of Tic-Tac-Toe.

REDUNDANCIES, REDUNDANCIES

There are a number of redundant phrases that have slipped into general use. Our emails and conversation are full of them. When crafting your writing, eliminate repetitive constructs and you'll sound fresh and avoid clichés.

When the second word has the same meaning as the first, choose one, or as often is the case, remove both and find a word that captures your meaning more effectively.

Compare this:

> *Each and every individual* needs to discover the *full and complete* spectrum of her *hopes and dreams* so that she can live a *very unique* existence free from the *true facts* of the *past memories* that affect her *whole entire* life.

With this:

> Discover your dreams to break free from your past.

Some other examples of redundant pairs:

basic fundamentals	future plans	true and accurate
end result	important essentials	unexpected surprise
final outcome	past history	various differences
first and foremost	sudden crisis	
free gift	terrible tragedy	

Sometimes the words don't say exactly the same thing, but one implies the other. Often, specific words imply their general categories. We don't need to state both.

Compare this:
> During that time period, many flamingos chose mates who were pink in color and unkempt in appearance.

With this:
> During that period, many flamingos chose pink, unkempt mates.

Some other examples of redundant categories:

at an early time	in a confused state
extreme in degree	large in size
heavy in weight	of an uncertain condition
honest in character	unusual in nature

DROP THAT

Sometimes entire phrases can be cut completely. Look for your use of the word "that"—often the phrase preceding it is a windup to your real idea, and can be trimmed out, leaving you with a stronger sentence.

Read these with the introductory that phrases:
>   We are of the opinion that fairies exist.
>   I believe that robots will control us all.
>   It's true that dolphins dream in technicolor.

Now read them again with the "that" phrase removed:
>   Fairies exist.
>   Robots will control us all.
>   Dolphins dream in technicolor.

Simple and powerful.

QUIT THE QUALIFIERS

Qualifiers are often used as fillers, and they don't add meaning. In fact, they do the opposite—soften the power of our words, weaken the impact of what we're saying.

Compare this:

> Simply because a great many of the words in this sentence are basically unnecessary, it would really be a very good idea to just edit somewhat for conciseness.

With this:

> Because many of the words in this sentence are unnecessary, we should edit it.

Or this:

> Edit this sentence—much of it is unnecessary.

Examples of Qualifiers:

actually	just	really
basically	kind of	somewhat
definitely	particular	sort of
extremely	practically	very
generally	probably	

LESS IS MORE

Many commonly used phrases can be replaced with single words. These circumlocutions take several words to say, when they could be said succinctly. You'll find you're left with a more natural rhythm to your prose.

Compare this:
> In the event that going out for the purpose of seeing the band's show with them cannot be avoided, it is necessary that we first go to the ATM, in light of the fact that I am thoroughly out of cash.

With this:
> If we must go see the band, we need to stop at the ATM. I'm out of cash.

Compare this:
> In accordance with your request, we have moved you to the Honeymoon Suite at this point in time.

With this:
> As you requested, we have now moved you to the Honeymoon Suite.

Some examples of words that can replace phrases:

About:
as regards
concerning the matter of
in reference to

Because, since, why:
considering the fact that
on the grounds that
owing to the fact that

Can:
has the capacity for
has the opportunity to
is able to

May, might, could:
it could happen that
it is possible that
there is a chance that

Must, should:
it is crucial that
it is necessary that
there is a need for

When:
in a situation in which
on the occasion of
under certain circumstances in which

DOWN TO SPECIFICS

The right word can hit like a bullet to a target. Sometimes writers settle for a shotgun spray, hoping at least one pellet will get close to what they were aiming for. This usually leaves the target in shreds. Choosing the right word can intensify the power of your sentence.

Compare this:

> The usage of a grouping of several words that are shorter and more difficult to fully discern can get in the way of energy and make it extra hard to comprehend the meaning of the sentence.

With this:

> Excessive and ambiguous words waste energy and thwart comprehension.

Compare this:

> Sarah liked Lindsey because she was nice and pretty.

With this:

> Sarah was drawn to Lindsey's easygoing charm and dark green eyes.

TO BE OR NOT TO BE

Look for verb forms of "to be" and "to have." These can often be replaced with strong verbs that are doing something, rather than just…existing. Remember that "to be" is an irregular verb, and shows up as:

am	being
are	is
be	was
been	were

Compare this:
> The peacocks are a positive element of our neighborhood.

With this:
> The peacocks improve our neighborhood.

Often we use "to be" in the form of nominalizations, where we transform verbs and adjectives into nouns. Used too often, they'll make your writing sound stuffy and abstract. Find the active verb that's disguised in the nominalization, and use it as the main verb.

Look for sentences that begin with:

There is
There are
This is
That is
It is

Compare this:
> There is a need for further investigation into her crime spree.

With this:
> We must investigate her crime spree further.

In an active sentence, the subject—the person or thing doing the action—comes first.

I wrecked the car.

In a passive sentence, the object—the thing that is receiving the action—comes first, and the subject appears at the end of the sentence, or not at all.

The car was wrecked by me.
The car was wrecked.

Once again, we're looking for forms of the verb "to be"—if it's next to another verb, especially one that ends in -ed, it's likely passive voice.

was lost
was damaged
is being chased

Passive voice often ends up as word clutter, and it can frustrate a reader, who has to untangle who or what did the action of a sentence. Turn passive voice sentences into active voice by getting rid of the "to be" verb and putting the actor back into the sentence.

Compare this:
> The fool is pitied by me.

With this:
> I pity the fool!

IN DEFENSE OF PASSIVE VOICE

We don't want to demonize passive voice altogether. Here are a few times when we recommend passive voice:

When it is more important to draw our attention to the person or thing acted upon.

Example:
> Two cups of chickpeas are added after the mixture has reached a boil.

Example:
> My nephew was cast in a film.

When it's not important to know about the actor in the situation.

Example:
> Shooting stars can be observed nightly over the skies of Big Bend.

When the writer wants to avoid placing blame or taking responsibility.

Example:
> Mistakes were made.
> Wine cooler ads were designed to appeal to teenagers.

Everything in moderation, even "to be" verbs.

WE'RE HUNTING HABITS

Often the words and phrases you'll want to replace don't necessarily follow any grammar or style rules—they're the ones that you default to, overuse.

Choose some words or phrases you feel yourself using often, and search your document for them. How often do you use the words "sure" or "unfortunately" or "similarly"? How often do you use "And just like that" or "Later that same night" or "he said, shaking his head sadly"?

Some words—"just" is a great example—can often be simply deleted. For others, you'll want to assess how often they appear, and revise some so your writing feels fresh.

Think also on your sentence structure. You might find that when you want to punctuate a moment you use a long meandering sentence followed by a snappy two-word sentence. Sometimes this will be sharp and powerful. But used too often it'll feel repetitive and forced.

Like a punchline that was funny the first three times, but the fourth time lands flat, at a certain point, the word, phrase, or sentence structure feels tired and weak.

Take the time to discover your patterns, habits, and defaults, and you'll find your way to crisp, clean, engaging writing.

ONWARDS

For me, writing is a basic tenet of life.
Food, water, love, writing.
So it's not that I have to make time for writing, it's that I have
to allow myself to not feel guilty because I have to write.

K. A. Holt

ARE YOU FINISHED?

OWEN

It was Ben who said it. "These pages are bruised."

He was referring to Will's opening chapter of his novel. Beautiful pages we'd read and he'd revised over and over… perhaps too many times.

How does a baker know when he has kneaded the bread the perfect amount? How does the gardener know to stop watering? How does the painter know to put the brush down?

You don't. Not really.

I've seen Tim O'Brien reading from one of his published works pause and make a mark on the page—a change for the next printing. Walt Whitman famously edited and added to the same book throughout the second half of his life, leaving several versions of *Leaves of Grass* for readers to argue over. Though many agree his edits to his original poems, including "Song of Myself," seldom strengthen the work. Kerouac, on the other hand, subscribed more and more to the philosophy of First Thought, Best Thought. But some of his later novels, many feel, hungered for the craft of revision.

There are two extremes—one is the *overworked novel*. A piece that has had the life pressed out of it like a peach too firmly gripped. You put so much of yourself into a book. But that self is ever-changing. I often take five years to write a novel. The person who begins that novel is not the person who finishes it. We—the me of now and the me of five years before—are perhaps close enough friends to collaborate. But if there's too much time, that relationship becomes strained. I could never write my first novel now—

that's just not me. If I were still, fifteen years later, working on that novel, I'd change everything. I'd be an awful collaborator. I'd put the me of now into it. And at some point one must let go. Press send. Leave it to the readers.

The other fault is the *undercooked book*. This is the work not yet ready, ideas not yet developed. Not because of a lack of effort, necessarily. Often because of a lack of time. The menacing friend of the gardener, wine maker, and writer. Some ideas and stories just need time to rise. We've all read undercooked books. Often the second or third work of a young, celebrated writer. Someone the publisher is encouraging to finish. As luck would have it, publishers are rarely begging me for my next book. I can take my time. But, ah, the demands of wild success. Trusted editors promise, "It's fine, fine. And we can have it in stores by Christmas." And the book comes out of the heat with mush under the crust.

A work will tell you it is done, but if you are like me, it will tell you more than once. Like a child declaring she is now all grown up, a manuscript is convinced (and will try to convince you) that it has grown to maturity and is ready to face the world. Our job is to listen, skeptically.

But there comes a day, all too late for some and much too early for others, when it is time to let the book go, allow it to be, give it the freedom to go toward the final important rite of passage for any book—not being written, but being read.

GENIUS MEATBAG

JODI

After the stark revelation that I am (probably) not going to win a MacArthur Foundation Genius Grant—you know, the one that gives you $625,000 to, basically, go on being your genius self—I found myself deep in the thick of an existential crisis.

I heard it on NPR—one of my college classmates was among the newest crop of MacArthur Geniuses. And here I was, driving my car—okay fine, my minivan—in my yoga pants, and my mom ponytail, heading to pick up my kids from school.

And that's when it hit me: I've plummeted past forty, and I still don't know what I want to be when I grow up.

I thought back through every career-related life decision—I should have listened to my AP Bio teacher who told me to go into neuroscience. I should have tried out for *Saturday Night Live*. I should have studied engineering, or computer programming, or…whatever it is that earns people income.

But. Still in my minivan, I turned onto Brodie Lane and had an equal and opposite startling revelation: I am a hermetically sealed bag of meat and bones, propelling a hunk of metal down a stream of flattened dirt on a giant rock ball zooming around a fireball in the midst of vast nothingness. And I'm sentient! Meat and bones, strung together in a tidy sack, somehow able to walk and talk and think. I mean, it's amazing I can even put pants on myself when you think of the complicated interplay of ligaments and armature.

So what now? Do I just say, "Well, I'm alive, that's enough!?" Do I still try to seek rewards, untold riches, and an occasional Pulitzer? I can spiral down and back up again in a moment, deep in the thick of the Genius Meatbag Conundrum.

I don't have an answer. I'm not exactly sure what it all means, and I'm certainly no closer to a Genius grant or existential enlightenment. But I'm choosing to enjoy my spins on this rock ball, choosing to spend my time sharing all of my favorite words, and maybe, just maybe, adding a little bit of extra joy to the world.

PRAYER FOR WRITERS

Dear God,

Spare a blessing for the writers.

We have traded in the bars and bullfights for university jobs and Netflix. We sink into credit card debt awaiting publication, then find the advance won't cover the monthly interest. Oh Lord, the books that took us years and blood have the shelf life of warm goat milk. In desperation, we write zombie erotica ebooks under false names, outselling our life's work 10 to 1. Our friends and family flip through our drafts, shake their heads, and return to their games of Candy Crush.

In the midst of all this, may we be writers.

May we grieve and sin and celebrate all in the same swallow.

May we seize morning light and squeeze it into ink and toner.

Grant us coffee and honesty and laptops that do not connect to the internet.

Teach us to be chefs, plucking herbs from sidewalk cracks and mushrooms from basement floors. And if we fail to provide nourishment for the hungry, may we at least offer the aroma of cooking.

We are starving, God. Every last one of us.

May we persevere remembering Emily Dickinson, John Kennedy Toole, and Henry David Thoreau. That said, God, we'd like the timing to be a little kinder in our case.

Deliver us, oh Lord, from the temptation to once again check our Amazon ranking or Google our own name.

May we write books worthy of being banned, outrageous enough to be burned.

May we offend.

May we be open to the wisdom of our colleagues and know when to forget every voice but our own.

May we visit the hearts of pedophiles and tour bus conductors and volunteers working suicide hotlines.

May we sneak into the funerals of strangers.

May we run mad so we may write for the mad. May we face brokenness so we can give voice to the broken.

A little happiness would be nice as well.

May we remember that how we live is essential to how we write. And refuse to live small.

Stoned or sober, may we piss in the pools of wealthy neighbors, eat in bars with health code violations, and steal bibles from homeless shelters.

May we make love loudly, even when alone.

May we embarrass, embarrass, embarrass ourselves.

May we be lost. May we pen maps so others might become lost as well.

May our greatest risk not be our words but our lives. And may our lives spill words like molten rock.

Damn the writers, God. Then bless us with the words to describe it.

If I sound ridiculous it is because I am ridiculous. This is my religion. This is my faith.

God, cast your gaze upon us. See us in the kitchens, closets, coffeehouses. Sitting and scribbling, typing, staring off between words. We raise our souls like a sloshing glass of grain alcohol. We toast one another. We smash the glass and light a match.

Forgive our clichés. Heal our poor grammar. And thank you, dear God, for Spell Check.

Oh Lord, hear our prayer.

Amen.

ACKNOWLEDGEMENTS

This book would never have come into existence without the support of our 332 Kickstarter backers. Thank you for encouraging us, trusting us, supporting us, and cheering us on. It's been a blast to craft this book for you.

Researching the book, writing the essays and exercises, launching *The Write Up* as a KUT podcast, and exploring our thoughts on creativity has been a true honor that you made happen.

Special thanks to these Kickstarter backers:

Chris and Sarah Walters, Gareth Egerton, Madeline and Ed Friedenthal, Scott Sherman, Brett Sherman, Lisa Efron, Derrick Amoriko, Alisa Miller, Amanda Krauss, Amy Estes & Tobin Scroggins, Angela Briones, Anne Marie Hampshire and Tom Pearson, Ashley Vena and Nader Afshar, Bernie and Pam, C. Robert Cargill, Clay Nichols, Cori Gerlach, Dawn Lindsey, Dayne & Leigh "Owen Married Me" Choate, Evan Thayer, Fran McHugh, George Bendele & David Welch, Gregg Charalambous, Haven and Chris Mass, Heather & Ruston Vickers, Jam Sanitchat, Jason Neulander, Jeffrey Travis, Jerry Aubin and Kerry Joyce, Johanna Gilmore, Joy & Brian Standefer, Julie Harms, Lauren Sheppard, Manning Wolfe, Max & Gabi Everett, Melissa Joulwan, Michael and Devra Prywes, Muna Hussaini, Nancy Thomas, Neil Wilson, Rebecca Drysdale, Rebekah Gainsley, Rosalie Tharp, Sarah and Trae Stanley, Shelby & Nicole Spradling, Susan B. Anthony Somers-Willett, Terry and Barak Benaryeh, The Gibbs Family, The Lieneck Family, and Theresa and Kenny Trice.

Thank you to our writing community, including the readers and revelers of the One Page Salon, BookPeople, the Texas Book Festival, Michael Noll and Read to Write Stories, *American Short Fiction*, *The Austin Review*, A Strange Object, Lucky Dark Press, The Writers' League of Texas, Bethany Hegedus and The Writing Barn, and Wendy M. Walker and Awst Press.

Thank you to Andrea Couch Wofford, graphic designer extraordinaire, for the cover design and layout.

Thanks to our eagle-eyed proofreading team, Anne Marie Hampshire, Arden Yingling, and Beth Eakman. Sorry, Anne Marie, that we insist on using the Oxford comma. But we're right.

Much thanks to the Khabele School and Primavera, the Alamo Drafthouse, Master Pancake and the Fancakes, the Typewriter Rodeo, CreativePickle, Epicenter, Liz Parker, UTA, and the Blackberry Smashers.

Endless thanks to our beloved family—all the Shermans, Walters, Egertons, Taylors, Friedenthals, Camargos, Lofthouses, Dayers, Efrons, Starks, Silvermans.

Gratitude to the best parent team any couple could imagine, Roz and Jeff Sherman and Judith and John Egerton.

Love and artichokes to our finest inspirations, Arden and Oscar.

ABOUT THE AUTHORS

Jodi and Owen Egerton live in Austin, Texas, with their two fantastic kid-dos, Arden "Boy Wonder" Egerton and Oscar "Tricky Machete" Egerton, a leopard gecko named Iapetus, guinea pig sisters Piggy Stardust and Poppy Diphthong Egerton, and six vintage typewriters.